PET HEROES

Extraordinary Acts of Courage and Devotion

Lisa Wojna

FOLK
LORE
PUBLISHING

The Publisher: Folklore Publishing
Website: www.folklorepublishing.com

Library and Archives Canada Cataloguing in Publication

Wojna, Lisa, 1962–
  Pet heroes: Extraordinary acts of courage and devotion / Lisa Wojna.

  Includes bibliographical references.

ISBN 978-1-926677-68-2

  1. Pets—Anecdotes. 2. Animal heroes—Anecdotes. I. Title.

SF416.W65 2010   636.088'7   C2010-902514-8

Project Director: Faye Boer
Project Editor: Kathy van Denderen
Front Cover Images: © 2006 Hemera Technologies; Photos.com
Back Cover Image: © Jupiter Images

We acknowledge the support of the Alberta Foundation for the Arts for our publishing program.

We acknowledge the financial support of the Government of Canada through the Book Publishing Industry Development Program (BPIDP) for our publishing activities.

 Canadian Heritage Patrimoine canadien

Dedication

To Pudd—a long-standing and faithful feline
who has never asked for much more than a belly
rub and who loves unconditionally.

Contents

Acknowledgments

OUR PETS HAVE A DEPTH OF CHARACTER that deserves recognition, and a book like this would never exist without this acknowledgment. To that end, I owe a debt of gratitude to Koda and Chance, Lulu and Faith, Bubba and Scarlett and every one of the dozens of animals included in this book. Some of them are working animals. Others are community companions. Every animal depicted in these stories is or was a beloved pet. And each of these brave creatures was so smart, so concerned and so faithful that despite the fact that humans haven't always been kind to them or recognized their great worth, they have garnered all their abilities and acted heroically. On behalf of animal lovers everywhere, I say "thank you."

Writing might be a solitary occupation, but putting together a book such as the one you are now holding never is. Most of the stories told here, although described and relayed in my own voice, were originally shared in countless media outlets around the world. I'd like to recognize and thank all the wonderful journalists, broadcasters, bloggers and communicators everywhere who were the first to share these stories with the world.

I'd also like to thank my wonderful editor, Kathy van Denderen, who took my initial chicken scratch and made sense out of my meanderings, reining in these tales and bringing them to life in the way they appear today. I've had the privilege of working with Kathy many times, and this experience was as enjoyable and magical as those preceding.

Thanks to Faye Boer, my publisher, mentor and friend. You give me the great gift of variety, and I can hardly wait to see what's in store for me in the future!

Thanks to my long-suffering husband, Garry, who supports everything I do; to my wonderful adult children—Peter, Melissa, Matthew and Nathan. And to my darling five-year-old Jada who, by now, is not only used to her mother sitting for long hours at the computer but is also old enough to bargain for "special time" once a project is finished. Thank you for your patience, Jada—Mommy will make it up to you! And last, but certainly not least, thank you to my beautiful grandson, Seth. Without you all, this and anything else I do would be meaningless.

Introduction

Some people come into our lives and quickly go. Some stay for a while, leave footprints on our hearts, and we are never, ever the same.

–Flavia Weedn, writer and illustrator

THROUGHOUT HUMAN HISTORY, animals have been viewed as our helpmates. We've ridden on their backs, harnessed their power and instructed them to plow and taught them to protect. We've also raised, fattened and consumed them, or draped their skins around our bodies or on our floors. In short, animals have served their two-legged companions in every way imaginable and, for the most part, until fairly recently, that's what we expected them to do. Nothing more.

Of course, that doesn't mean we don't appreciate the efforts of our fellow creatures. Nor does it overlook the affection we feel for our pets. But in recent times it's become increasingly clear that our animal friends are so much more than creatures that are smart and teachable. These furry friends have a depth and worth of their own. But recognizing the worth of animals and their rights has been a hard-won battle for the people who care for them.

Public and government views of animals as recent as the 17th century was summed up by Nicholas Malebranche who once stated that animals can "eat without pleasure, cry without pain, grow without knowing it; they desire nothing, fear nothing, know nothing." French philosopher René Descartes echoed this sentiment, arguing that animals have "no souls, minds, or reason," and although they can hear, touch and eat, he did not believe they had any "conscience," as we define the word, and were "unable to suffer or even to feel pain."

Although Descartes might have echoed the general public sentiment of the time, the topic was obviously heated enough that it continued to generate discussion among philosophers of the day. Thankfully, those early academic arguments have, like human morality, evolved. In the last hundred years or so, more and more governments the world over are publicly recognizing that animals have basic rights that include the right to live, the right to "freedom" and the right to "personal safety." We now recognize that animals feel pain. We know they are smart and feel emotion. For example, I just need to spell the word "W-A-L-K" and my two shelties go crazy, and if I dare leave the house without them, they whine and, in some cases, jump at the kitchen door in frustration.

The collection of stories in this book outline how faithful, loyal and steadfast our pets can be. Pets have been credited with recognizing that their owners were sick, sometimes long before their owners did. They've risked life and limb to save the person they loved. Pets have traveled thousands of miles to reconnect with a lost master. And they've mourned their master's loss to paralytic degrees, at times even beyond death.

From the many tales of animals risking their own safety to rescue a family member from a burning fire, to the fierce and fearless dogs credited with protecting children from rattlesnakes, to elephants that can sense a tsunami on the rise, to the parrot who warns its owner about an intruder, to police dogs risking their lives so their handlers can go home to their families at the end of the day, these stories prove that, yes, absolutely yes, pets are more than mere animals.

They are kindred spirits.

Part One

THE BEST OF FRIENDS

We long for an affection altogether ignorant of our faults. Heaven has accorded this to us in the uncritical canine attachment.

—George Eliot, writer

THE DICTIONARY DEFINITION OF a friend is someone with whom you have feelings of attachment, or a sense of knowing and trust, and to be a friend requires a person to become an ally and provide support or assistance wherever and whenever needed. Interestingly, most official definitions put a "person" on the giving or receiving end of friendship, but I'd venture to suggest those are fairly narrow uses of the term. Animals can and have been friends to humans since the dawn of time, whether we've recognized it or not. They've attached themselves to their human caregivers, demonstrated endless affection and offered their assistance whenever they sensed a need.

In short, these animals we call our "pets," which according to the same dictionary simply means "a domesticated or tamed animal that is kept as a companion and cared for affectionately," are our friends in every sense of the word.

The stories that follow demonstrate friendship in the truest form. Some stories deal with animals that have sensed something was wrong with their master, or another member of the family, and provided support to their loved one. Other stories show how some animals extended the meaning of "friendship" to include humans outside their friends and family, how they reached out to help a stranger in distress.

All of these stories demonstrate the noble qualities every hero possesses.

Dogs, Dogs, Dogs

A person can learn a lot from a dog, even a loopy one like ours. Marley taught me about living each day with unbridled exuberance and joy, about seizing the moment and following your heart. He taught me to appreciate the simple things—a walk in the woods, a fresh snowfall, a nap in the shaft of winter sunlight. And as he grew old and achy, he taught me about optimism in the face of adversity. Mostly, he taught me about friendship and selflessness and, above all else, unwavering loyalty.

–John Grogan, *Marley and Me*

Zulu, the Missing Martyr

My little dog—a heartbeat at my feet.

–Edith Wharton, writer

THE BLACK RANGE MOUNTAINS of New Mexico's southwestern corner are largely composed of cliffs and mounds of sedimentary and metamorphic rock that spilled into the area in the form of magma thousands of years before its first human inhabitants ever arrived. The rugged canyons of the southernmost portion were once inhabited by the Mogollon people more than 700 years ago. Early in its history of human settlement, this region boasted all kinds of gold and silver mines, but today, this sanctuary is retired from the world of mining and turned into a national monument. It's a land rich in story; it's also a land abounding in natural wonder. And in a very busy world, it's the perfect place to hike into the wilderness and spend an afternoon lost in the beauty of it all.

You can get a lot of sunlight in the Black Range Mountains during the month of November, but the warmth of the sun's rays can be deceptive; they don't necessarily translate into mild nights. So when 67-year-old Robert Sumrall lost his way in the evening hours of November 28, 2009, and didn't make it home by the time it grew dark and temperatures plummeted, his family was more than a little concerned. They were outright frantic.

An Ordinary Hike

Hikes through the Black Range were something Robert Sumrall took fairly regularly. Sumrall was enthusiastic about his planned outing; his walking companion that day was a little less thrilled at the prospect of a backwoods adventure, though.

Three-year-old Zulu, a small black Labrador-cross, was more of a homebody than an avid hiker. The youngest of the Sumralls' three dogs was born on a lazy July day in 2006, and the Coronado Hills neighborhood where the family lived was her home. Zulu's mother, a golden Labrador named Lucy, had several puppies over the four years she was part of the Sumrall family, but Zulu was a special pup that captured their hearts, and when the rest of her siblings were adopted out, she remained.

Zulu's softhearted nature revealed itself immediately. Her personality evolved as steadily as her little body developed in her first few weeks of life. It was clear she was a softie—Zulu wouldn't likely live up to the stalwart image of the Zulu people she was named after. In fact, according to a story told by Jan Sumrall, Zulu once backed down from the family's cat.

Nevertheless, when the El Paso, Texas, resident decided to go for a planned hike at Emory Pass in the Black Range Mountains of neighboring New Mexico, Robert decided that of the family's three canines, his companion for the Saturday outing would be Zulu. The pup had only been out with Robert hiking once before, and Zulu was overdue for a second trek. A day hike seemed like the perfect outing for the inexperienced dog. Still, the canyons in November can be dangerous. Weather conditions change rapidly, and you need to be prepared for anything.

The Emory Pass is just one of several hikes the area has to offer, and trails often branch off from one another offering climbers a choice between shorter day excursions and overnight backpacking adventures. Sumrall had no intention of making it an overnighter when he left the Emory Pass trailhead and began walking south, but when he came across an old mine and couldn't find the trail leading to Iron Creek, he started losing time. After searching for the trailhead for nearly two hours, Sumrall eventually found himself in Bull Trap Canyon and up against some craggy terrain.

At one point, he had to carry Zulu, who could have never scaled the large, six-foot-tall boulders that blocked the path. But in his efforts to climb the obstruction, Sumrall slipped and fell, tumbling, dog and all, into a large puddle of water. Now they were not only lost but they were also wet, and the distinct chill of early evening air stuck to their bodies.

Despite his earlier intentions to take only a day hike, Sumrall surrendered to the reality that he would not be making it home that night. Quite aware of how cold it can get in a canyon once the sun has set, Sumrall was determined to make it to the top of the nearest mountain. Once there, he built a fire and tried to dry his clothes as best as he could. Exhausted from the day's undertaking, Sumrall finally fell asleep, sandwiched between the fire and Zulu and with nothing but a thin, solar blanket shared with his wet pet for added warmth.

The next morning, Sumrall was pretty sure his family would have contacted the authorities and formed a search party, but since he had no idea where he was, he felt he needed to keep moving. He also had no food, save a few power bars, and limited clean water. He was growing increasingly tired with every passing hour, and the last thing

Sumrall wanted to do was spend another night in the cold.

Unfortunately, that's exactly what happened. After spending the day and the better part of the evening traveling along Little Gallinas Canyon, with Zulu dutifully following her master, the pair found themselves with no shelter at all, aside from a few trees, and so they huddled together in an effort to shield each other from the wind.

The cold was only one of Robert's worries; there was also hungry wildlife to consider. Although most of the area's bear population were in hibernation for the winter, it was possible that a few stragglers were still up and about, actively looking for their last meal. Bears might not prefer to feast on people or dogs, but they can get a little testy when they feel threatened!

Mountain lions were another consideration—and a mountain lion can bag a moose if it's hungry enough. It promised to be a long, cold, nerve-wracking night, and the knowledge only served to exhaust the senior further. Surely, he thought, help was on the way.

That night, temperatures dipped to around freezing. Add that to the wind chill and Sumrall, dressed in nothing more than shorts and a sweat-shirt, may not have lasted the night without Zulu snuggling warm and close. Over the next two days, just over nine inches of snow fell. Sumrall's situation was becoming more desperate by the moment.

Two Down, Four to Go

The next morning, reflecting on the previous day, Sumrall realized he had come to his current location because he'd heard what he thought was the sound of machinery in the distance. He suspected there might be people nearby, and so he passed through two locked gates and continued in the direction from where he thought the sound was coming. But after his restless night, Sumrall thought twice about his earlier decision because he did not come upon anyone. He decided to retrace his steps through the two locked gates and onto the horse trail he'd been following the day before.

Sumrall likely questioned his own eyes when he saw a cabin in the distance: was it a hopeful dream, like a mirage on the desert? The closer he got, he could see it was a ramshackle affair, but it was real nonetheless. Best of all, the most comfortable-looking lawn chair was set out in front of the building. Sumrall sat down—after a while it just feels good to sit on something besides the cold, hard ground.

After resting for a few moments to gather up as much energy as he could, Sumrall got up and approached the cabin door. It was locked. No problem, he just happened to be carrying a .357 magnum pistol. Shooting the lock several times, the senior blew it open, only to find he now needed to wrestle with the door itself. Eventually, he managed to pry it open, and on seeing a small sofa inside, Sumrall collapsed on it in exhaustion. Zulu curled up on the floor, almost as tired as her master. Sumrall's lighter wasn't working, and he couldn't focus long enough to check out every corner of the cabin in search of matches, so he couldn't make a fire. There was one saving grace, however. Fresh water was available in a cistern outside.

There wasn't any food in the building so Sumrall and Zulu shared the last energy bar. Sumrall could feel his stomach twist and turn in hunger, and he could only imagine how Zulu felt, but his dog didn't whine or become agitated over the situation. Instead, Zulu stuck close to Sumrall's side.

Still, Sumrall knew that help had better come soon or both man and beast would succumb to starvation or hypothermia. Sumrall was grateful for the shelter he had found, but it was far from warm in that ramshackle hut. Without a fire, it was only slightly warmer behind those thin walls than it was outside.

Another day dawned. And then another. At this point, the days just blended into each other, and Sumrall wasn't sure how many nights he'd spent in the wilderness. But what he did know was that he didn't have any more energy bars. He was faced with the reality that he'd have to leave the shelter of the cabin soon, or both he and Zulu would starve to death.

Sumrall was also thirsty, so Zulu must have been, too. Focusing on their most immediate need, Sumrall left the cabin to get water from the cistern. That's when his eyes landed on the lawn chair he saw when he first came across the cabin.

"I remember thinking, 'That sure was a comfortable lawn chair,'" Sumrall later told reporters from
the *Silver City Sun-News*. "I sat down in it, and that's the
last thing I remember, until vaguely waking up in
University Medical Center (in El Pasco). I was probably within a couple of hours of just being gone."

The Search Continues

While Sumrall was going through his own personal hell, the rest of his world was overwhelmed
with worry over the man's well-being. His family had
reported him missing Sunday morning, but it took
some time to organize any kind of search. Once the
man's car was located at the Emory Pass trailhead,
several volunteer search and rescue teams were called
in, and their efforts were coordinated with the New
Mexico State Police. But it was snowing—an accumu-
lation of as much as 10 inches from Sunday night to
Tuesday seriously hampered rescue operations.
Visibility was limited. Tracks were covered and
eventually erased by the moisture, which also threw
search dogs off the scent trail.

There was also a bit of confusion among the rescuers over which direction Sumrall had gone. At first,
authorities believed he was traveling on the more
northern trails of the Gila wilderness. However, on
Wednesday, after Sumrall had been missing for
four days, someone Sumrall had spoken with on
Saturday morning provided additional evidence
that resulted in a search farther south. No matter
how anyone looked at the situation, the whole rescue

attempt was starting to feel as though they were looking for a needle in a haystack. With more than 770 square miles of hinterland in the Gila National Forest, choosing which direction the man took relied heavily on educated guesswork.

People also started debating whether the senior could have possibly survived the cold so long, especially without any food. Surely if the conditions were so bad that rescuers had to limit their efforts because of blizzard-like conditions, Sumrall's chances of survival were decreasing by the minute. Sumrall's daughter, Paige, was quick to address these concerns, saying she was confident in her father's ability to cope. "If anybody could have lasted this long out there, that's my dad," she told reporters from the *El Paso Times*.

While the search efforts were continuing, Sumrall's body had melted into the lawn chair in front of the cabin, and he lost consciousness. His unsupported weight eventually toppled the chair to the ground. With a whimper of concern for her master, Zulu moved closer and crawled on top of him, keeping him warm and protecting him from the elements.

It's not clear how long Sumrall was unconscious on the ground, but on day six of his ordeal, ranchers Melba and Tom Parra were on their way to round up cattle and happened to pass near the cabin, which was located near Royal John Mine Road. It was Friday, December 4. The weather was typically cool and, sensing how important it was to keep her master warm, Zulu was still curled up by his side. Melba and Tom knew right away what they'd come across. The couple had heard the news stories about a man and his dog who'd gone missing in the area, and only moments earlier, Melba had been thinking about the man's plight.

"When I saw him, I just knew right away that was him," Melba told *Silver City Sun-News*. "He wouldn't have survived another night out there...I guess God must have put us over here for him."

The couple rushed to the man's side. Sumrall was clearly confused, mumbled for water and asked to hold the woman's hand. Melba could see he was very cold—surprisingly, he was wearing a pair of jeans and a light jacket, which was more than he had been wearing when he left on Saturday. Clearly he'd managed to bring a few supplies with him, but there was still no way he was dressed warm enough for the weather.

"I think the only thing that kept him alive in this cold was this black Lab," Melba told reporters. "She was laying next to him. He was really cold."

While Tom turned back for help, Melba stayed with Sumrall and tried to raise his body temperature by putting a jacket on him and curling up to him to try to share her own body heat. With the arrival of the two strangers, and the flurry of sudden activity, Zulu became spooked and ran off. Thinking the dog would eventually return, Melba focused her attentions on Sumrall. But when rescuers arrived, and the missing senior was transported to University Hospital in El Paso, it was clear another problem had to be solved—what had happened to Zulu?

Rescue Efforts Resume

When Robert Sumrall finally emerged from his coma, and his condition elevated from "critical but stable" to a far more hopeful assessment, he told of how Zulu protected him, without a single complaint, throughout the entire experience. Sumrall knew the dog was every bit as hungry as he was, but she never left his side. Instead of searching for something to eat, Zulu had snuggled up next to her master. She was his protector throughout the ordeal and his warmth on those cold nights. Zulu was also his company, and she propelled Sumrall to stay focused and not give up.

According to the Sumralls, that Zulu existed was a bit of a miracle itself. The family had adopted her mother, Lucy, from the El Paso Animal Rescue the day before the shelter was planning to euthanize her. Shortly after Lucy had settled into her new home, it became evident that the Sumralls hadn't adopted just one dog—Lucy was carrying a litter of puppies!

Zulu was one of the 11 pups Lucy eventually gave birth to, and Robert's granddaughter, Emma, chose Zulu as her own. The eight-year-old was clearly devastated by the loss of her dog, and every day since the dog's disappearance, she asked whether anyone had located Zulu. But Emma was master in name only.

Unable to keep the dog at her home, Emma was content knowing that Zulu would live with her grandparents. At more than three years of age, the dog had spent every night sleeping at Lucy's side. Zulu wasn't just any dog. Everyone who knew her saw her as a shy, timid creature, and they worried about her safety. Even Lucy paced the house in her nightly ritual of looking for her pup. Clearly, Robert wasn't the only one concerned about the dog.

While Robert was recovering, family members and volunteers involved in the original search once again combed the area where Robert had been located. Bowls of food were used as bait. Paige, and her step-sister, Wendy, also searched the area, bringing hot dogs and a favorite toy to bribe Zulu. The dog's story had captured the hearts of dog lovers across the country. The *El Paso Times* reported how people from El Paso to New York had "fallen head over heels for Zulu." A fund was set up to help offset costs associated with the rescue efforts, as well as to establish a monetary award that, a few days after Robert had been found, had already grown to almost $3500. The Sumralls pledged a $1000 reward to anyone able to bring Zulu safely home to them. Everything possible was being done to find the faithful canine.

Although the Sumralls were concerned that Zulu did not have what it took to survive the cold and the wilderness for very long, veterinarians interviewed about her odds of survival seemed to give the pup a lot more credit. They pointed out that her size was a positive asset, suggested that she should be able to hunt for small game and explained that a dog could conceivably go without food for two weeks if need be. And most importantly, the drive to survive is any animal's biggest motivator.

With a substantial reward offered, the Sumralls received several false reports about Zulu being captured. On the other hand, there were alleged sightings, including some video footage collected by one Silver City resident who hunted in the area. It was thought that Zulu was traveling through the places she and Robert had hiked together, returning to Emory Pass and making a loop with each turn.

Waiting and Wondering

As the days progressed and Robert's health recovered, life returned to normal for most of the people involved in this story. For the Sumrall family, however, nothing would be the same until Zulu was found. In March 2010, Robert's story was again featured on the pages of the *Silver City Sun-News*; keeping Zulu's plight in the public eye is necessary if Robert is ever to be reunited with his hero. Robert has also pledged to regularly return to the area in the hope that one day he'll spot Zulu.

Animal lovers with an ear for this story haven't forgotten Zulu either. The Humane Society of El Paso and the Animal Rescue League bestowed the title of "hero" on the dog in an official ceremony on April 9, 2010.

Zulu was the first animal to receive this particular distinction, but Robert doesn't need the honorable recognition for him to know his beloved Zulu is a hero. The man will never forget those seven days of hell, nor will he forget the bond he shared with one special black beauty. For Robert, Zulu is a hero of the most honorable kind—one that would give up her life for her master.

As of this writing, Zulu has not yet been found.

Bringing Comfort

Good instincts usually tell you what to do long before your head has figured it out.

–Michael Burke, journalist

THERE WAS NO SOUND. NO commotion to capture his attention. No strong scent in the air to alert him to any concern or danger, and yet Brett Grinde's German shorthair, Effie, was acting strangely. The normally well-behaved dog was out walking with Grinde during the late-afternoon hours of Monday, January 11, 2010, when she started pulling on her leash. Grinde tried to correct his anxious charge, directing her in the path of their regular route, which was in the opposite direction to where Effie wanted to go, but she continued pulling to the right.

Pets who behave out of character usually raise the curiosity of their owners, especially pets who've been around as long as 15-year-old Effie. After much persuasion on Effie's part, the Pine City, Minnesota, man finally unclasped Effie's leash, but he ran close behind his pet, concerned at her erratic behavior; after all, she wasn't an unpredictable teenager anymore.

As a Pine County sheriff's investigator, Grinde recognized that Effie was urgent in her quest; he knew instinctively that something was wrong. With her nose pressed to the ground, Effie rushed some 50 yards away, stopping in the driveway of a nearby home. Grinde followed Effie as closely as possible.

"I ran after her, and when I turned into the driveway, I couldn't believe it," Grinde told reporters from the *Minnesota-St. Paul's Star Tribune*. There, laying face down on the cement driveway in a pool of blood was 94-year-old William Lepsch.

With almost three decades of police service under his belt, Grinde flew into automatic. He checked the man's airways and started CPR while Effie licked the elderly man's face. Eventually, the dog lay down beside the fallen man as Grinde worked from the other side. After a while, it appeared the man was regaining consciousness.

Meanwhile, Lepsch's wife, 88-year-old Marjorie, was breathing a sigh of relief from the window of the couple's home. She had a good view of the driveway and noticed that her husband had fallen sometime after 2:00 PM that day. Marjorie later told reporters that William hadn't mentioned that he was leaving the house so she wasn't sure how long he'd been outside before she saw him. Marjorie, who relied on a wheelchair and a walker to get around, couldn't leave their home to help her husband of 67 years, and she struggled even to get to a telephone.

By the time Grinde arrived on the scene, and before Marjorie had managed to call her niece, the elderly woman was hoarse and exhausted from her efforts at attracting attention.

Emergency personnel arrived on the scene soon after, and the man was transported to North Memorial Medical Center where he was treated for broken ribs and hypothermia. Investigators later surmised that the gentleman had left the house either to take out the garbage or pick up the mail, and in the process, must have slipped on the ice. Sadly, William did not survive his injuries.

Despite the sad outcome, Effie was no less a hero in the eyes of the Lepsch family or in the eyes of her master. Effie's keen sense that something was wrong and Grinde's decision to follow his dog's lead gave an elderly man some dignity in his last hours and allowed the people who loved him most a chance to say goodbye.

A Worthy Companion
Is the Biggest Hero

God, grant me the serenity to accept the things I cannot change, the courage to change the things I can, and the wisdom to know the difference.

–Reinhold Niebuhr, theologian

WILDWOOD'S CACTUS THORN isn't the name of some type of bush or plant, it's the handle of a cream-and-brown dachshund with several unique talents and one severe handicap. In early 2007, the pup was one of a seemingly healthy litter, but by the time he opened his eyes and visited the vet for his early checkups, it was clear Cactus had a pretty major problem. Cactus was born blind.

His blindness could have resulted in the pup being euthanized, but when Bob Gabbard saw the beautiful creature, he couldn't pass him by and let fate take its course. After all, to some degree, Gabbard could relate to Cactus' situation. For years, the Tulsa, Oklahoma, man struggled with a circulatory problem in his right leg, which in time resulted in its amputation. Gabbard got around his house and yard with the help of a scooter or wheelchair; he knew what it was like to live with a physical challenge.

Gabbard decided to take a risk and adopt Cactus. And a risk it surely was because the gent wouldn't have the ability to chase after the pup if the need arose. Gabbard knew he needed to be diligent in Cactus' training regime.

As fate would have it, Cactus was an obedient and smart dachshund. As Gabbard explained to KOTV news reporters, the pup learned to compensate for his lack of vision with his ears and nose. His hearing and sense of smell were so well developed that Cactus quickly grasped the layout of Gabbard's home and mastered the limitations in the man's backyard. Cactus also learned to respond to a whistle.

But more than that, Cactus' sheer determination and high spirits are infectious. These qualities infuse the people around him with an indescribable joy. Thanks to Cactus, Gabbard has a companion that is loyal, loving and so much fun.

"When he enjoys life as much as he does, it helps all of us enjoy our lives a little more," Gabbard told reporters.

Clearly, Cactus recognizes his limitations and enjoys life despite them, sharing his enthusiasm with everyone he knows. Now that's nothing short of heroic.

Against All Odds

Dogs have given us their absolute all. We are the centre of their universe. We are the focus of their love and faith and trust. They serve us in return for scraps. It is without a doubt the best deal man has ever made.

—Roger Caras, American wildlife photographer

THIRTY-NINE-YEAR-OLD DANELLE Ballengee is no stranger to pain. She's an extreme adventure athlete and long-time personal trainer who competes in a combination of mountain biking, paddling, hiking, climbing, running and navigation during any one race event. She's the kind of competitor who never gives up, and she reaps the rewards of her efforts.

During one adventure race, which took place in the year 2000 in Borneo, a remote island located north of Australia, Danelle managed to finish the event even though a leech had attached itself to one of her eyes, leaving her blind for three days after the event. She stumbled across the finish line dehydrated after completing a 46-mile desert run in 105° F heat, a run she completed without any water for the final four hours. She'd run with torn ligaments and blistered feet, and come out a winner after completing races that left her unable to stand at the finish while at the same time earning herself a first place. And despite these and many other difficulties, Danelle accumulated a long list of personal achievements that included six U.S. Athlete of the Year awards in various adventure sports.

As it turned out, the events were all only dry runs for the real race—the race to save her life.

Of course, she had some help in this adventure—a little four-legged help that went by the name of Tasman, or "Taz" for short.

A Gentle Run
The idea of taking a run through Utah's backcountry might seem challenging for novice athletes, but for extreme sports enthusiasts, the area offers up a plethora of challenges that can raise the adrenalin at any given time.

Moab, Utah, is an especially alluring location for folks who love to exercise in the great outdoors. Nestled in a green oasis just south of the Colorado River, the city is surrounded by a stunning, red rock landscape chipped out of the earth's surface and preserved through the governing of several national parks. It's a haven for lovers of the outdoors, and the area so intrigued Danelle, who in 2004 was named the "world's greatest female adventure racer" by *Sports Illustrated*, that she purchased a home in the city.

Moab is a small community, to be sure, with a population of about 5000. But what it lacked in numbers and in the many amenities that come with more populated centers it more than made up for in opportunities for wilderness experiences.

That's what Danelle thought, anyway. And so in early December 2006, she packed up the few supplies she usually took with her on a "short" run, collected her pooch, loaded her truck and readied herself for a run around the glorious landscape of the Hurray Pass, just outside Moab. It was ironic that on that fateful day, Danelle wasn't planning anything daring. This trek was supposed to be a quick two-hour run; Danelle regularly did events that were a thousand times more daring than this, and she had every intention of making it home in time for lunch.

Initially, the run went along as planned. Taz was enjoying his workout too, running close by Danelle at some points and rushing ahead at others. And then the unthinkable happened. About halfway through the run, Danelle's foot slipped on a patch of black ice, pummeling her down a 60-foot canyon. She hit one rocky ledge after another, until she finally landed at the bottom.

Stunned by the sudden descent, it took Danelle a few moments to gather her thoughts and react as the well-trained athlete she was. Beginning with small efforts to move her toes and then her feet, she discovered she wasn't paralyzed. Breathing a sigh of relief, she then tried to lift herself off the ground. The excruciating pain searing through her body soon put a stop to that idea. She might not have been paralyzed, but she had certainly broken something. In time, she also recognized the signs

of internal bleeding through her growing and dis-
tended belly. Still, she knew she had to inch her
way out of the canyon before nightfall. For five
agonizing hours, with a worried Taz who'd found
his way down the mountain and was now by her
side, she painstakingly pulled herself a scant quarter
of a mile before exhaustion overtook her—she was
stuck there for the night.

Although she'd halted her efforts to crawl back
to her truck, Danelle knew she had to keep moving
in order to keep her blood circulation flowing
through her body. She performed a slow and steady
succession of modified crunches. She scooped
small capfuls of water into the water bottle she'd
emptied on her run, but only allowed herself the
occasional sip to avoid the need to urinate. She
found an energy gel in one of her pockets and ate
that. She called Taz over to her and nuzzled as
close to him as she could to keep her lightly clad
body from succumbing to the 20° F temperatures
and eventual hypothermia.

And so it was that Danelle passed that first night
and then a second. Throughout the entire ordeal,
Taz remained by her side. His very presence likely
warded off any potential predators. His body
helped take the edge off the cold nights. But by
Friday morning, Danelle knew she had to send Taz
away. She had to tell her faithful companion to
find help—she could only pray that Taz understood what she was asking him to do. If he failed to

deliver, Danelle knew there was little hope she'd survive another night in the cold.

Serendipity at Its Best

While Danelle was struggling to survive and hoping someone would eventually come to her aid, her neighbor started to wonder where the young woman had been hiding the previous two days. On Thursday afternoon, Dorothy Rossignol, Danelle's neighbor, finally called Danelle's parents in Evergreen, Colorado. After checking all the likely places where their adventurous daughter might have disappeared, and not being able to locate her, they called the police.

"With all of the things Danelle does, we didn't really want to bother people and make a big deal of it if she was just out training. But we just had a gut feeling that we needed to do something, and thank God we did," Peggy Ballengee told reporter Brian Metzler of ESPNoutdoors.com.

After ruling out any kind of foul play, police started searching the areas where Danelle normally trained. And on December 15, they discovered her pickup at the Amasa Back trailhead.

John Marshall was the officer responsible for directing 12 members of the Grand County Search and Rescue team into an organized search party tackling different portions of the wilderness where Danelle's truck was discovered. He decided that several teams would ride through the most likely trails that Danelle might have run on. But before anyone had the chance to set these plans in motion, Taz came into the picture.

At first, rescue workers thought that perhaps Taz was a wild dog, but after watching him edge his way closer to workers only to get their attention and then rush off, they changed their minds and acknowledged it was quite likely that the dog was indeed Danelle's trusty running companion. The sight of the animal sent Marshall's pulse up a few beats. "Most dogs won't leave their master as long as their master has a pulse," Marshall told Devon O'Neil of the *Summit Daily News*. "To see that dog was a truly saddening sight."

According to Grand County Sherriff's Office chief deputy Curt Brewer, several attempts to catch the dog were unsuccessful. Taz would venture just close enough to get everyone's attention and then turn back in the direction where Danelle lay cold and injured.

"The search crew decided to follow the dog," Brewer told ESPN. "And the dog took our rescue personnel right to her [Danelle]."

At 3:38, on the afternoon of December 15, after spending 52 hours cold and injured in the unforgiving climate of the Moab wilderness, rescuers found Danelle. After she was transported by helicopter to St. Mary's Hospital in Grand Junction, Colorado, medical personnel discovered that Danelle had fractured her pelvis in four places. She suffered other minor injuries, as well as the internal bleeding she'd suspected, but she was alive.

In her own words, Danelle later shared her experience in TrainingRx.com. She told of how Taz "cuddled up next to [her] providing some warmth." She described how he "knew something was really wrong by now," and how she told him she "loved him and asked him to go get help." She shared how watching Taz "running up and down the canyon, returning to check on me every so often" had made her cry. And she recounted how that last time that Taz returned, she felt a rush of hope, and when it was confirmed that her beloved companion did indeed manage to get help, the tears that filled her eyes brought her the first warmth she'd felt for days.

Taz seemed to know the trauma was over too. He "wagged his tail and sounded a whimpering cry of joy as he licked" the hand of Danelle's rescuer. "I was given a second chance for life," Danelle wrote of her account.

That second chance was due, in a large part, to the efforts of one very loyal canine.

An Odd Match Softens a Crusty Heart

People who keep dogs live longer on average than those who do not.

This is not some kind of pro-canine campaigning fantasy. It is a simple medical fact that the calming influence of the company of a friendly pet animal reduces blood pressure and therefore the risk of heart attack.

–Desmond Morris, British zoologist, ethnologist, painter and author

LIKE MOST BREEDS, DACHSHUNDS attract a certain kind of personality. You can picture a large, burly fellow paired with a bulldog or a Rottweiler, while a Papillion or a Lhasa Apso might be more befitting a woman of genteel disposition. That said, being a rather small creature, a double dapple dachshund pup with a snarly plumber known for his cranky disposition isn't a pairing that would first come to mind.

Then again, that's exactly what happened to Bobby Hollabaugh of Amarillo, Texas.

What's more unbelievable is that even though Bobby's family loves him, his wife, Glenda, and the couple's two grown sons can't get over the change in Bobby since Toey came to live with the family in the fall of 2004. However, the breeder who brought the small dog to the Hollabaughs' home on a hunch probably knew this special pup was exactly what Bobby needed to smooth out his rough edges.

The day he first laid eyes on Toey, Bobby didn't need a formal introduction. When Bobby's breeder friend brought her over, the first thing Toey did was anxiously check out her new surroundings, ambling directly over to Bobby and nibbling on the man's toes. The audacity of the little monkey melted Bobby's heart, and in case you hadn't figured it out by now, the dog's initial interaction with her new owner landed the pup with his name—Toey.

Toey didn't come without a few concerns, however. It was clear from watching the pup make her way across the kitchen floor that she was blind. Bobby suspected that if he didn't adopt the pup, the breeder might be forced to put the dog down (a lot of communication can sometimes take place when no one is talking, but everyone is paying attention).

The silent dialogue and unspoken realities of Toey's situation resulted in Bobby finding himself with a new companion. From that day on, the pup and master spent the majority of each day together—whether Hollabaugh is at home, at work in his shop or in his truck, Toey is right there, preferably on her master's lap.

It wasn't long before Bobby recognized that something else was wrong with Toey. Sudden, loud noises, like a car backfiring, didn't spook her, and she didn't respond when called. The man, who when his kids were young was so harsh as to suggest his son be moved to the front of the class to deal with poor vision, marched right over to a veterinary specialist to have Toey's hearing tested. Sure enough, Toey was clinically deaf.

If words don't adequately explain Bobby's feelings for his dog, his actions clearly show his affection for Toey. While at one time Bobby refused to allow a dog in the house, today his beloved dachshund not only gets to stay on the bed but also sleeps under the covers. But even more than just loosening Bobby's household rules, Toey has managed to soften an otherwise crusty gent and, in the process, has made life so much more enjoyable for everyone around him.

"It's changed his life," Glenda told Jon Mark Beilue of the *Amarillo Globe News*. "He used to be a grouchy old man, and now the dog has turned him into the biggest baby...I can't tell you how much he loves that dog."

Of course, Glenda isn't left out of the picture completely as far as Toey is concerned. In fact, Bobby would argue that he plays second fiddle to his wife, even though she disagrees. Glenda loves being Toey's mama, but when the pooch senses that Bobby is getting ready for work, she bolts off Glenda's lap and rushes to her master's side.

Some might feel sorry for Toey for missing out on seeing and hearing so much of the world's beauty, but she enjoys every moment of her life. The Hollabaughs do everything they can to make her life warm and comfortable, but Bobby is quick to point out that it is truly more blessed to give than to receive.

"That dog has done me more good than I have her," he told Beilue. "She's kept me calm and kept me sane."

Chance Gives Boy
Only Hope for Survival

True benevolence or compassion extends itself through the whole of existence and sympathizes with the distress of every creature capable of sensation.

–Joseph Addison, English essayist

IT SHOULD HAVE BEEN A HAPPY TIME. With Christmas only weeks away, most children were writing out their wish lists, dreaming about opening presents and planning that first Christmas morning run-through with all their new toys. They were excited about gingerbread cookies and candy canes, visits from grandma and a two-week holiday from school. For most children, their biggest worry was trying to discern if they'd been naughty or nice that year.

On Saturday December 5, 2009, James Delorey had a few other, more pressing matters on his mind. At around 2:00 PM, the seven-year-old, thrilled with being alive and having a great time playing outside, trotted out of his family's yard in South Bar, a rural community about six miles north of Sydney, Nova Scotia, and steered himself into the nearby woods. James and his dog, Chance, had been playing with the boy's mother, Veronica, up until that point. But Veronica had been alerted that the family's motor home had started rolling down the hill it was parked on, and she rushed to the vehicle to secure the brakes, leaving James and Chance alone for just a few seconds. When she returned to where they'd been playing, James and Chance were nowhere to be found.

Veronica was panic-stricken and ran into the brush calling after her son and the dog while winding her way along several pathways she thought they might have traveled. When it became clear she wasn't going to find the truant twosome, Veronica called in the police. It was a frightening situation, but Veronica recognized one small glint of sunshine in the blackness—the family's nine-year-old Dalmatian-cross was with James. Although Chance wasn't a trained service animal, the dog had a close attachment to James. Chance recognized when James was worried or anxious. He had a calming effect on the child, and he was fiercely protective.

The innocent adventure probably seemed like a good idea to the youngster, but it wasn't long before the cold, damp weather typical of the northernmost tip of Canada's Atlantic province at that time of the year started to turn James' skin into gooseflesh. A bitter wind was gaining momentum, adding a sharp chill to the air. While Veronica was talking to police and helping organize a search party, the lad, who had left his home wearing nothing more than jeans, a plaid shirt, sneakers and a light, gray vest, hugged himself tighter for extra warmth. By the time evening fell, James was more than just a little cold. He was quite literally freezing.

And he was lost.

Bad Turns Worse

A missing child, especially someone as young as James, always kicks emergency responders into high gear. Even though police had no reason to suspect that this was an abduction, and it was clear from the beginning that the youngster had purposely wandered off for a bit of fun and got lost, the situation was urgent. The police and James' family were worried that he might hurt himself in the woods, might come up against some of the area's wildlife or, because he wasn't wearing a hat, mitts, coat or any other warm clothing, might fall victim to hypothermia. In addition to these concerns, the Cape Breton Regional Police, the volunteer search and rescue workers and the members of the public who turned out in droves to help locate the missing child had yet another worry to deal with: James was a child with special needs.

According to several Sun Media news reports, this wasn't the first time James had wandered away from the safety of his home, but his tendency to do this wasn't about his wanting to get away or escape from a bad situation. One mental health worker explained to reporters that wandering was a common behavior for children like James who were diagnosed with autism. Perhaps this is why James' dog followed close behind the meandering child and stayed by him through his entire ordeal. It was as if Chance knew James shouldn't be alone; he knew the boy would be scared and cold and lonely if he became lost.

While Chance stayed right beside James, trying to provide a measure of warmth and comfort to the frightened boy as he lay underneath a thicket of spruce trees, rescue workers were battling challenges of their own. The weather, for one, was not cooperating. A rescue helicopter equipped with state-of-the-art night-vision gear was on standby, but it had been grounded because of a storm that was brewing over the Atlantic and moving inland. Wind gusts of up to 40 miles per hour added an icy bite to the already frigid temperatures, and a heavy fall of wet snow reduced visibility and made conditions hazardous for all aspects of the search effort.

By the next day, concern for James' welfare turned frantic. Cape Breton Regional Police spokesperson Diseree Vassallo said that although searchers were looking for the lost lad, the weather was continuing to worsen, and everyone was wet and cold. As much as six inches of snow had fallen over the previous 24 hours, making foot travel through the swampy, wooded area even more difficult for rescue workers. And although searchers called to the boy and his dog, it wouldn't necessarily produce the desired results unless James could see them and run their way. That's because even if James was still conscious and otherwise responsive, he couldn't speak—he wouldn't be able to alert rescuers to his position and condition. And if he did happen to hear rescue workers calling out to him, James might misread their intentions and flee from the very people who were trying to save him.

Hundreds of people were involved in the search for James and his dog, along with a pack of canine officers, manned all-terrain vehicles and boats and a wide variety of special equipment. But with the cold, the snow, the wind and the damp unpredictable swampland as well as the Atlantic Ocean being just a stone's throw from where James had wandered off, the outlook for his rescue was becoming increasingly dim.

A Light in the Darkness

By Monday afternoon, the thread of hope everyone was holding onto that James would be found alive was becoming more and more tenuous.

And then the unthinkable happened. Chance came home!

The dog ambled out of the woods with the single-minded goal of making it to the Deloreys' house, and the media heralded Chance as the "lucky break" that rescue workers were looking for. Following the dog's footprints back to where they originated, rescue workers discovered James where Chance had left him, underneath the thicket a mere mile from a command post that rescue workers had set up. The boy was in very poor condition; his body temperature had dropped below 95° F, securing a diagnosis of hypothermia. In that state, his small body wasn't able to regulate its metabolism or adequately manage its temperature or circulation or keep his organs in good working order and maintain other bodily functions.

Looking back, it was as if Chance knew he had to take a leap of faith and do something he'd never done before—leave the boy and try to find help. It was, in effect, James' last hope if he was to survive his ordeal. And so the dog made the tough decision to leave James' side.

While searchers were excited to find James, their enthusiasm was short-lived when they discovered his condition. "Our fingers are crossed," Emergency Health Services spokesman Paul Maynard told reporters from Quebec Media Inc. "Hopefully a miracle will happen, and he will pull through."

It took two hours for rescue workers to find James, and another 90 minutes for paramedics to arrive and get the boy stable enough to fly him to the IWK Health Centre in Halifax, the leading pediatric hospital in the province. The Deloreys were given their child back, if only for a while, but they couldn't give up hope.

From Miracle to Angel

To hear James' mother speak to the media about the peace of mind she received knowing Chance gave her boy some measure of comfort during the 48 hours he was lost and cold reminds us that, as William Blake once wrote, "joy and woe are indeed woven fine." The show of support from the community, Chance's decision to look for help and the mere fact that James' parents didn't have to spend the Christmas season or longer wondering what had happened to their son—Veronica gave thanks for all these things.

But it didn't take away the sting of what would eventually become the end of the story.

Young James died the next day. His small body just could not overcome the effects of the hypothermia. Christmas was evolving into a season of sorrow for the Delorey family, and on Monday, December 14, hundreds of people packed a local church to show support for James' parents and his two siblings and to pay their last respects to the youngster. Chance was also at the service, having been awarded a place of honor in the front seat of the hearse as the funeral procession made its way to Cape Breton's Holy Redeemer Church.

Reverend Errol MacDonald saluted the efforts of the small community of people who put planning for Christmas aside in order to elevate the meaning of the season through their collective sacrifice of time and love to help a family reunite with their little boy.

"This is the busiest time of the year. Everyone is caught up with their own agendas," MacDonald told mourners that day. "Yet in the past week, everybody stopped. And in that stopping they found the true meaning of Christmas—that a child would give us hope." Reverend MacDonald reminded mourners that although James passed away, there was indeed a Christmas miracle in his story and that "he turned into a Christmas angel."

As a final gesture of grief, emergency workers and search volunteers who attended the funeral were the last to file past the boy's coffin and place a spruce cutting on top. James did not live to see Christmas that year, but his service ended with a chorus of Christmas carols.

In some ways, saying good-bye to James at his funeral was the final chapter to a very sad story. But area residents weren't about to forget the one they considered to be the real hero of the story.

And they were about to act, in a big way.

A Show of Gratitude

Purina has had a long history in feeding animals top-quality food since 1893, and while the company has evolved and changed over the years, one thing has remained consistent: its commitment to the animals it serves. Every year since 1968, the people at Purina PetCare have inducted worthy animals that have demonstrated "extraordinary acts of heroism and bravery, which have saved human lives," into the Purina Animal Hall of Fame. The stories behind this annual recognition range from pets that have saved their owners from a wild animal, alerted them to a house fire or raced for help when their owner was in some type of physical distress. To date, 140 animals have been so honored, and of that number, 125 were dogs, 25 were cats, and one was a horse. In 2010, Chance became one of those honored animals.

Chance, like the 139 other animals on the Purina wall of fame, showed his mettle by putting his young master first and conducting himself throughout James' ordeal in an orderly fashion, denying himself and doing everything he could to help provide the boy with warmth, comfort and later some long-awaited assistance.

But what sets Chance apart from every other animal on that registry is the sheer number of people who thought the dog special enough to nominate him to the Purina Hall of Fame. More than 400 nominations poured in for Chance.

James may not have survived, but in the eyes of a community, Chance was no less the hero for his actions.

Hope Abounds in Desperate Situation

*Hope is that thing with feathers that perches in the
soul and sings the tune without the words and never
stops...at all.*

–Emily Dickinson, poet

A TRAGEDY THAT OCCURS DURING the Christmas season is
doubly harsh; a triumph at that time of the year
is double the joy. That's certainly how Donna Molnar
and her friends and family felt in December 2008
after Donna disappeared one afternoon.

The three-day episode that had an entire community out searching for the missing 55-year-old Ontario
woman started on the afternoon of December 19
when Donna left the couple's home in Ancaster to
pick up a few supplies for some Christmas baking.
David, knowing his wife had stepped out to do an
errand, didn't worry until the early evening. As the
temperature began fluctuating and a storm started
brewing overhead, David decided to call police and
ask for their opinion on what to do.

That first night was an excruciating journey for
David and his son, Matthew. The two men tried to
figure out where Donna might have gone, but they
didn't have any luck in finding her or her vehicle.
It wasn't until the next evening when a police car
on a routine patrol passed by Lindley's Farm and
Market, located on Fiddler's Green Road in a rural
area outside of Ancaster, noticed the woman's SUV.
By then, the hunt for the missing wife and mother

was gearing up. Now that the police had a reasonable idea of Donna's last-known whereabouts, search and rescue workers and other emergency personnel could focus their attention on the area where the Molnars' vehicle was found.

Of course, the weather stops for no one. Emergency situation or not, snow continued to fall the entire weekend. Two huge snowstorms were recorded, each dumping about one foot of snow and effectively covering any tracks that might have assisted in the search and making it difficult for anyone to wade through the neighboring fields with any precision.

Back at the Molnars' residence, Matthew and David were overcome with worry. Christmas had been a tough season of late. Donna's mother and father-in-law had both passed away at that time of the year, and the thought that the Molnars could lose Donna as well was overwhelming.

The Search Continues

Hours turned into days, and there was still no sign of the missing woman. Even some of the most optimistic searchers started to worry that they were now on a recovery mission instead of a rescue. Along with the heavy snowfall, temperatures dipped as low as 59° F during the night, and 50-mile-per-hour winds only added to the weather's brutal sting. When she'd left her home, Donna was wearing a simple winter coat; she likely wasn't expecting to be wandering about in a snowstorm. The prognosis wouldn't have looked good for anyone caught outside in those winter conditions for as long as Donna had been gone.

David and his son were bracing themselves for the worst.

By Monday, December 22, Ray Lau and his volunteer rescue dog, a Dutch shepherd named Ace, joined in the search for the missing woman. The dog and handler, who were a relatively new partnership and still getting to know one another, focused on combing a farmer's field across from where Donna's SUV had been located. Lau later told reporters that he had every expectation that he was searching for a body, so when his dog suddenly took off, he had mixed feelings about what he would discover. While inching his way to the spot where Ace had stopped, and was endlessly barking, Lau prepared himself for what he might find.

"There she was, there was Donna, her face was almost totally covered except for one eye staring back at me," Lau told reporters. "I couldn't believe she was still alive."

It took rescue workers quite some time to extract Molnar from the two feet of snow packed down on her body, but it was because of that snow and the insulating effect it had that, according to officials, likely saved the woman from a cold and lonely death.

But she wasn't out of danger yet.

The Long Road Home

While rescue workers carefully excavated the woman from her snowy tomb, Donna apologized for causing so much trouble. She'd just wanted to take a walk, she told members of the Hamilton Police Department. She seemed surprised to discover she'd been away from home for three full days and expressed concern over her husband and son. That selfless attitude, the way Donna had of always putting the other person first, was typical, David said.

Although she was lucid and could carry on a conversation, Donna's body temperature had dropped to a dangerous 86° F. Her extremities were also frostbitten, and medical personnel were concerned that she might be faced with necessary amputations. Regardless of the medical outcome of the saga, David was just glad to have his wife back. To anyone who would listen, David called Donna his "Christmas miracle." It was as if "God reached down and cradled her in His arms until they [rescue workers] found her." To Donna, he simply said, "Welcome back, I love you."

It took 11 long months of around-the-clock hospital care before Donna was well enough to return home. David had to sell the family's house and purchase another home that was wheelchair accessible and able to accommodate Donna's new special needs. Following her ordeal, Donna had to deal with the eventual amputation of her hands and feet, as well as a stroke that she suffered the week after her rescue.

The road ahead continues to offer up countless challenges for the Molnar family. But were it not for Ace and his keen sense of smell that drew him to a minute impression in the snow that Christmas season in 2008, they would have never had the opportunity to heal.

Remarkably, the assignment was Ace's first as a volunteer rescue dog, and he shattered everyone's expectations. The dog that was once considered a difficult pup and surrendered by its original owner had bonded well with his new master. Together Ace and Lau will have a relationship that promises more success stories in its future.

In the meantime, Ace was named the Service Animal of 2009 in the Purina Animal Hall of Fame.

Feisty Felines

With their qualities of cleanliness, discretion, affection, patience, dignity, and courage, how many of us, I ask you, would be capable of becoming cats?

—Fernand Mery, *Her Majesty the Cat*

Ty, the Love Muffin

A cat has absolute emotional honesty: human beings, for one reason or another, may hide their feelings, but a cat does not.

—Ernest Hemingway, writer

CATS ARE AFFECTIONATE, INTELLIGENT and free-spirited animals that love their owners but don't need to be coddled; Siamese cats are perhaps more like this than some other breeds. Those who are familiar with the Siamese variety of feline would likely agree they're more extroverted than other kitties, and it's not uncommon for Siamese cats to be thought of as possessing sensitive, sometimes even nervous, temperaments.

This description might explain why on a particularly hot July night in 2004, Ty was a little fidgety.

It was easy to see how the unusually plump and stocky Siamese was named after heavyweight champion boxer, "Iron" Mike Tyson. The eight-year-old Siamese was a bruiser with a bit of an attitude. He did, however, have a distinct soft spot for his mistress, 66-year-old Myrna Birch. Myrna was equally enamored with Ty, often calling her fluffy friend the "Love Muffin."

That July night, the resident of Trail, BC, was having a hard time sleeping. Myrna's air conditioner wasn't working too well, so at about midnight, the agitated woman decided to get up and feed her cats that, it appeared, were having an equally difficult time getting comfortable for the night.

No sooner had Myrna stood up than she felt the room spinning, and then everything faded to black. As Myrna later told reporters from *The Province* newspaper, "the lights went out."

It was Ty who took notice of his mistress' distress; it was Ty who didn't give up on her. Instead of slipping off with his littermates, Ty hovered over Myrna's lifeless body, yowling and growling, licking her face and even pawing at it from time to time. "I kept coming in and out of consciousness because Ty was licking my face and my eyes and my nose and screaming in my ear, just hollering his head off," Myrna told reporters. "I would come to and then I would hear this horrendous roaring in my head and then I would pass out again."

Ty's persistent pestering roused Myrna enough that the retired industrial nurse recognized she was in big trouble. During those brief moments of consciousness, Myrna tried to pull herself in the direction of her telephone. But she didn't get far before she passed out again. As soon as she did, Ty was back at it, licking her face and howling some more. Finally, after about two hours of drifting in and out of consciousness and dealing with Ty's assiduous nagging, Myrna was able to grab her telephone cord and pull the phone onto the floor. With her next bit of energy, the woman dialed 9-1-1.

By the time paramedics arrived, Myrna's heart was taking its last beats. Emergency personnel had a hard time registering any blood pressure whatsoever, and her heart was struggling to beat 20 times a minute. She was shipped to Kootenay Boundary Regional Hospital, and shortly afterwards, Myrna had a pacemaker implanted.

From the moment she first heard Ty's haunting yowling and realized what was possibly happening to her body, Myrna knew there was only one reason why she survived. Without Ty's determination and concern for his mistress, Myrna would have died before help ever arrived.

"[Ty] recognized right away that there was something horrendously wrong. If he hadn't been persistent and kept at me, I would have just slowly slipped away. He kept me going," Myrna told reporters. "He is a love muffin..."

Ty was heralded a hero for his efforts and was one of three animals inducted into the Purina Animal Hall of Fame in April 2005. The big boy was carted around in a limousine, awarded a medal and certificate recognizing his efforts and provided with food for a year. Myrna was thrilled with the honor bestowed on her special cat. Ty, on the other hand, wasn't too bothered about it all. In true hero style, only one thing mattered to him, and that was the safety and well-being of his favorite person.

Baby Monitor

One reason we admire cats is for their proficiency in one-upmanship. They always seem to come out on top, no matter what they are doing, or pretend they do.

—Barbara Webster, die-hard cat lover

ON APRIL 17, 2006, REUTERS NEWS AGENCY reported a strange story out of Cologne, Germany. A family was awakened by their cat's persistent howling, and no amount of hollering outside the window managed to shut it up.

When the homeowner finally decided he'd had enough and made his way outside to check on his cat, he found it rubbing itself against an interesting package left on the front doorstep. Surprised, the man bent over and had a look inside and found one very alive, very cold baby boy. Had the cat not continued to howl and the man not roused enough to go outside before the morning, the baby could have been in dangerous condition.

The newborn was rushed to the hospital at 5:00 AM and, miraculously, suffered little more than a mild case of hypothermia. Exactly who the baby belonged to remains a mystery, but there was one thing everyone involved in the story agreed on: the noisy cat was the hero of the day.

~❊~

On a Clear Day

The cat could very well be man's best friend but would never stoop to admitting it.

—Doug Larson, journalist

A DOG MAY BE A MAN'S BEST FRIEND, but canines don't corner the market on animal loyalty. Cats might be more reserved in showing affection, but they know the important people in their lives. Even after years of separation, a cat will recognize a master who once cared for and loved it.

Such was the case for Susan Skillen of Scotland. Her cat, Saffy, disappeared in 2004 but was found six years later and was returned to Skillen. Although Saffy was emaciated and unkempt, she reportedly bound into Skillen's arms. "I think she's really happy to be home," Skillen said.

~❊~

Other Critters We Love

The difference between friends and pets is that friends we allow into our company, pets we allow into our solitude.

–Robert Brault, freelance writer

The One and Only Lulu

I like pigs. Dogs look up to us. Cats look down on us. Pigs treat us as equals.

–Winston Churchill, British prime minister

THE MORNING OF AUGUST 4, 1998, dawned soft and warm along the southern shores of Lake Erie. The lazy days of summer had arrived, and Jack and Jo Ann Altsman were looking forward to a restful time away from the stresses of everyday life.

The couple, who lived in Beaver Falls, Pennsylvania, was entering their golden years, so no youngsters were tagging along. Still, they didn't travel alone. Bear, an American Eskimo dog, and Lulu, a Vietnamese pot-bellied pig, happily accompanied their master and mistress on most outings. This vacation was no exception.

Jack had planned an early-morning fishing trip with his buddy that Tuesday, and Jo Ann was content to remain in bed for a few more hours. Determined to find himself a fishing hole that might supply him with the catch of the summer, Jack tossed a "See you later" Jo Ann's way and rushed out to meet his fishing partner.

A couple of hours after Jack left, the alarm clock went off—rest and relaxation was one thing, but Jo Ann didn't want to sleep the day away. As she rolled over to silence the ringing, Jo Ann noticed she was dizzy. The sensation, followed by a searing pain radiating across her chest, knocked the wind from her lungs. She recognized what was happening—she'd been in this exact situation 18 months earlier. Panicking, Jo Ann knew she had to make her way to the telephone to call for help, or she might not have the chance to enjoy another vacation.

The phone was located on the other side of the room, so Jo Ann attempted to edge her way off the bed. Too weak to continue, she crumpled onto the floor. The sensation of panic now mingled with the squeezing tension radiating throughout her body, and Jo Ann sensed she didn't have much time before even the best in medical technology would no longer help her. Desperate, Jo Ann grabbed her alarm clock and hurled it through a window. She screamed for help, hoping someone might hear her through the jagged glass that remained. By now, Bear and Lulu had sensed that Jo Ann was in great distress and were showing their concern. But despite the added commotion of a yelping dog and a crying pig, the sounds simply drifted off into the Lake Erie wilderness.

There was no one around the Altsmans' Presque Isle summer home to hear the cries.

The Truth About Pigs

According to Dr. Bruce Lawhorn, swine expert at Texas A&M University's College of Veterinary Medicine and Biomedical Sciences, the common belief that pigs aren't too smart and don't form any attachments with their human caregivers is simply not true. Sources differ slightly, but most reliable reports suggest pigs are among the 10 smartest animals on earth. Although the Altsmans' dog couldn't contain his concern and continued yelping and whining, the couple's 150-pound porky pig tried to funnel her energy into doing something about the situation. Lulu, screeching and wailing with all the air in her lungs—a pig's screech can reach between 110 and 115 decibels, or as loud as a roaring jet but far more disconcerting—decided to waddle away. While Jo Ann writhed in pain on the floor of the mobile home, Lulu squeezed her way through the doggy door.

Now, if you stop to think about it, Lulu escaping via the doggy door was no small feat. Even if Bear was the largest breed of American Eskimo, he didn't measure wider than 19 inches at the shoulder and, in spite of a little extra weight, wouldn't have come anywhere near the 150 pounds his pig companion weighed. It is no wonder Lulu, crying her "big, fat tears" as Jo Ann eventually described to reporters, and howling the entire time, struggled to make it through the doggy door.

But where was Lulu going?

As Jo Ann called for help, and Bear yipped and yowled, Lulu made her way across the Altsmans' front yard, pushing open the gate and retracing the steps she'd walked on numerous strolls she'd taken with Jo Ann. Lulu was on a mission: intuitively, Lulu sensed that Jo Ann was in distress, and the pig was determined to do everything in its power to get her mistress the help she needed.

Of course, no one really stops and chats with a wandering pig. Unless you're a pig person, most of us wouldn't call out to it or try to pet the porker. There wasn't anyone around anyhow. So Lulu did what any smart pig would do: she made her way to the nearby road and waited to hail a passing motorist.

At least one report suggests Lulu's initial attempts weren't all that successful. Although she was on the roadway, waiting for a motorist to drive by, it appears not many vehicles passed her way. Jo Ann later learned that at least one confused motorist did stop for Lulu but found her presence on the road so unsettling that he didn't get out of the car. "She's not very attractive," Jo Ann told Michael Fuoco of the *Pittsburg Post-Gazette*.

At several points during her 45-minute ordeal, Jo Ann remembers Lulu returning to the cabin and making her way to her mistress. It was as if the pig was checking in on Jo Ann. "Somehow Lulu knew I was dying," Jo Ann told reporters from the UK's *Demand Five* TV. Although Jo Ann repeatedly tried to calm Lulu, telling her to "lay down" and go "night-night," Lulu continued her frenetic squealing. Then, after a few moments at Jo Ann's side, Lulu left again, forcing her way back through the doggy door and onto the road.

By now, Jo Ann had given up on any hope that she'd be discovered in time to receive medical help.

"I thought to myself, this is it. It's all over. I remember Lulu coming back, and I said for her to go as Mummy was dying. She went off again, and I just shut my eyes and waited for the pain to go," Jo Ann told reporters from *Erie Life Magazine*. Having lived through one heart attack, Jo Ann knew that with every passing moment her chances for survival were diminishing. She knew her heart was straining to pump much-needed oxygen-bearing blood throughout her system but that it was dying slowly.

Jo Ann was running out of time.

The Good Samaritan
Lulu, on the other hand, wasn't giving up. Her dogged persistence eventually paid off when one

gentleman, curious enough to stop his car, attempted to approach the pig. Once the man got out of his vehicle, Lulu sprang into action and waddled her way back down the trail she'd traversed several times by then, leading the young chap to the Altsmans' home. She would stop every now and again to turn and make sure the man was still following her.

Once the unlikely duo reached the trailer, the pig stopped. So did the man who was following her, quite sure that something was terribly wrong with this pig. Presuming the animal lived at the trailer, the young man opened the door and hollered inside, thinking he was alerting the owners that their pig was in distress. Instead, Jo Ann hollered back.

"I managed to find enough energy to shout back, 'So am I! Please call an ambulance,'" Jo Ann stated.

It was the miracle Jo Ann was waiting for. As the stranger made his way to the campground office to call 9-1-1, Jo Ann knew if she survived her ordeal, she had Lulu to thank. But as far as Lulu was concerned, her job wasn't finished. When paramedics finally arrived and were securing Jo Ann into the ambulance, Lulu continued to create a fuss. It appeared to everyone at the scene that Lulu wanted to accompany Jo Ann to the hospital.

Hero or not, Lulu didn't get to ride in the ambulance. Instead, she was transported to the nearest veterinarian to have her torn and raw belly cleaned and bandaged—the poor girl suffered several cuts pulling herself through that doggy door so many times. Needless to say, the Altsmans enlarged the doggy door.

A few days after her rescue, Jo Ann was transported to the hospital in Beaver Falls and underwent open-heart surgery. Her doctors told her that had another 15 minutes passed before help arrived, she would not have survived.

Lulu was the recipient of a whole lot of hugs—and a jelly doughnut—for her heroic efforts. Jo Ann never got to thank the Good Samaritan who followed Lulu from the roadside and called 9-1-1, though. Exactly who the young stranger was remains a mystery to this day, despite an earnest attempt by a variety of media outlets to identify the kind humanitarian.

Spreading the Word

Not one to keep her wonderful luck to herself, Jo Ann and Jack shared their story with their local newspaper, the *Pittsburg Post-Gazette*. The Altsmans most likely had no idea how widely their tale would travel. In a world full of sad news, the story of Lulu's exploits and Jo Ann's survival cheered the hearts of anyone who stopped long enough to hear it. Pretty soon, news agencies around the world were eager to produce their own unique rendition of the Altsmans' story for their readers and viewers. Lulu and her owners made an appearance on *Oprah*, the *Regis and Kathie Lee Show* and even the Japanese-based Nippon Television Network

Corporation. *Ripley's Believe It or Not* visited the Altsman home to cover the story—it aired on *Good Morning America* and *20/20*—and Lulu also had the opportunity to meet George Clooney when they both appeared on the *Late Show with David Letterman*.

Along with all the media attention, the American Society for the Prevention of Cruelty to Animals recognized Lulu with a gold medal for her heroic actions. And yet, with all this publicity, and an award offered for information about the unknown stranger who played a lead role in getting Jo Ann the help she needed, the identity of the Good Samaritan who called 9-1-1 remained anonymous.

What Goes Around

Life is full of juicy little twists of fate, and when it comes to the Altsmans' story, the fact they even had a pet pig was the biggest twist of all. You see, Lulu was never supposed to belong to the Altsmans. Lulu was bought in Edinboro, a borough in Erie County, Pennsylvania, the previous August. The four-pound baby porker, who was slightly over a month old at the time, was a gift for the Altsmans' daughter, Jackie, as her 40th birthday present.

It appeared Jackie wasn't overly interested in caring for a pet pig for what could conceivably amount to 30 years or more, and so when she returned home from a holiday, she never got around to collecting Lulu from Jack and Jo Ann, who'd agreed to care for Lulu during the time Jackie was away. As the days and weeks passed, the senior Altsmans grew more and more fond of Lulu, and pretty soon it was clear that the pig would remain with the couple. Looking back on it all, Jack told *People* magazine, "I know the Lord gave Lulu to us for a good reason."

Sadly, all did not end well for Lulu. On January 30, 2003, weighing at least 200 pounds over her recommended weight, the faithful and adoring pig died of a heart attack. She was five and a half years old.

In the end, it was her fame that did her in. Adoring friends and fans liked to sneak her treats now and again. The problem was that no one realized how many treats she consumed on any given day. While the Altsmans tried to strictly monitor her diet, Lulu was frequently found near the front gate of the couple's property, begging for treats from passersby. "She'd cry for people to feed her," Jo Ann told reporters. "She was the smartest, most special pig."

To honor the pig that saved Jo Ann's life, the Altsmans held a small ceremony for Lulu. Their loyal companion was lovingly placed in a trunk, along with her favorite Steelers blanket and assortment of stuffed toys. She was buried on a friend's farm as a handful of crimson balloons that Jo Ann and Jack released floated away into the sky.

At last report, Jo Ann still hasn't gotten over the loss of her beloved Lulu. Jack has suggested that they get another pet pig, but Jo Ann isn't convinced. Nothing will ever replace the determined pet pig who risked life and limb by sprawling herself across the road in an effort to commandeer help for her mistress.

For Jo Ann, there can only ever be one Lulu.

Parlez-vous Parrot?

Live in such a way that you would not be ashamed to sell your parrot to the town gossip.

—Will Rogers, entertainer

BIRD LOVERS LOOKING FOR A UNIQUE pet might consider the Quaker parakeet. Also known as the Monk parakeet, this bird is known for its charming disposition and love for its human buddies. This parakeet is also known for its considerable intelligence and pronounced ability to learn to talk. If you're planning to adopt one of these colorful creatures, there's one word of warning: you'd better keep your tongue on a short leash. These smart birds are well known for picking up words—a whole lot of words. In a relatively short time after their arrival in your home, you can expect they'll already have developed a large vocabulary. So if you're prone to spitting out some off-color words or mumbling to yourself about your eccentric neighbor, you might want to think twice about bringing this pet into your home.

It was a good thing that Denver, Colorado, resident Megan Howard wasn't worried about her tongue getting her into any trouble. She quite enjoyed the Quaker parrot she'd adopted and named Willie, and by November 2008, the pair had lived together long enough to develop quite a rapport.

That month, Megan was babysitting two-year-old Hannah Kuusk in her home and had set the youngster at the kitchen table with her breakfast. She then left the room to use the washroom.

Megan wasn't gone but a few moments when Willie started flapping his wings madly and repeating, "Mama, Baby, Mama, Baby," until the woman rushed back into the kitchen. Immediately, Megan noticed the cause of Willie's erratic behavior. Baby Hannah was turning blue and was in obvious distress.

Megan reacted on impulse, grabbing the young girl into her arms and performing the Heimlich maneuver. Later on, when Megan told Samantha, Hannah's mother, about the ordeal, she was overwhelmed with gratitude. Samantha told reporters that hearing about how her daughter turned blue makes her "heart [drop] in my stomach and I get all teary eyed," no matter how many times she hears the tale.

For Megan's part, she wasn't at all interested in taking credit for saving the little girl's life. Without Willie's frantic calls alerting Megan that something was wrong, the babysitter might have taken a few seconds longer to return to the kitchen—seconds that could have cost the baby girl her life. "[Willie] is the real hero," Megan insisted.

Apparently, others thought so, too, and on Friday, March 20, 2009, the noble bird was honored by the Mile High Chapter's "Breakfast of Champions." Colorado governor Bill Ritter and Denver mayor John Hickenlooper joined in on the celebrations, which eventually garnered so much press that notable publications, such as *People Magazine* and *Reader's Digest*, and even television personalities like Rachel Ray, covered the story. Megan couldn't have been more thrilled that her bird was recognized.

Like they say, great things sometimes come in small packages. Willie is certainly proof of the truth behind this old adage.

~∞~

Unlikely Pair Joins Forces to Save Master

Ideas are easy. It's the execution of ideas that really separates the sheep from the goats.

–Sue Grafton, mystery writer

SOME FOLKS DON'T KNOW THE meaning of the word "retirement." At least one could certainly argue that's the case with a 78-year-old Australian dairy farmer named Noel Osborne. The gentleman lived alone but was still able to manage his farm and care for his few animals, which included two he was particularly fond of: Mandy the goat and Mandy the border collie.

On the morning of Monday, October 8, 2002, Osborne was making his way around his property, completing his list of chores as he moved from place to place, when one of his cows did the unthinkable and lashed out, knocking the senior gent to the ground. His hip broke in the fall, and he was left in a potentially deadly predicament. Unable to move, and with no means of communication nearby, Osborne was stuck there and at the mercy of fate.

Regardless how bleak his situation might have appeared to the man, Osborne wasn't about to roll over and give up. A little later in the day, his pet goat Mandy happened to meander by and, noticing Osborne on the ground, ventured near to see what was the matter. Osborne had noticed an old bottle within his arm's reach and grabbed it, hoping he still had enough strength left to milk the goat and get a little nourishment.

His plan worked. Mandy the goat was quite accommodating, so much so that once Osborne had finished his task, Mandy knelt down and nestled in beside her master, providing him with a little warmth in the cool evening air. Not long after, Mandy the border collie also noticed something was amiss and made her way to Osborne's side. Flanking the farmer on each side, the two animals managed to keep him warm throughout the night.

As it turned out, they did that for quite some time.

For five long days and nights, Osborne lay in the exact same spot where he fell, using every ounce of his strength to call out for help. Mandy the goat continued to provide him with his only nourishment while Mandy the dog tried her best to bring him her own rendition of comfort food—old bones. The goat and dog duo were Osborne's only protection from the elements, and during those five days, he survived the cold nights and occasional storm with the warmth the two provided.

Days were a little more difficult to endure because they were hot, and aside from his two Mandys hovering nearby and throwing at least a small amount of shade his way, Osborne didn't have any cover from the sun. Still, as long as he could keep milking Mandy the goat, the farmer knew he stood a pretty good chance of surviving.

Osborne coasted through the first three days of his five-day ordeal fairly well, but by day four, his condition had weakened considerably, and he couldn't muster the strength to milk his goat. If help didn't arrive soon, Osborne could be in bigger trouble than he already was.

Finally, on day five, friends of Osborne stopped by the farm to pick up one of his kid goats and discovered the fallen farmer. They called in emergency personnel, and Osborne was transported to hospital.

The dairy farmer recovered in hospital, but he was well aware that had his two Mandys not faithfully watched over him, the outcome could have been quite different.

"I wouldn't have lived that long without the goat, especially in the weather conditions," Osborne later told reporters with the *Melbourne Herald-Sun*. "By cripes, I was lucky, wasn't I?"

Very lucky, indeed.

❧

Never Enough Credit for Horse Sense

And God took a handful of southernly wind, blew His breath over it and created the horse.

–Ancient Bedouin legend

HORSES HAVE HISTORICALLY PLAYED a huge role in human development. We've saddled them up and used them for transportation. We've harnessed them and used them to till the fields. We've outfitted horses for battle. And more recently, we've used them to bring comfort to patients struggling with physical and mental illnesses. Simply put, the horse has demonstrated several faces of heroism. But what's even more amazing is when this kingly creature deigns to stop grazing long enough to take notice of a situation and, unbidden, reacts on it.

Such was the case in the summer of 2007. Forty-year-old Fiona Boyd was making tea in her Chapmanton home, near Castle Douglas, Kirkcudbrightshire, England, when she heard a ruckus outside. The mother of two rushed outside, anxious to check out the cause of the commotion, and she discovered one of the calves had been separated from its mother and the rest of the herd. The calf was bawling uncontrollably. Fiona tried to gently urge it back to the shed, but by that time, the calf's mother noticed her offspring was in distress and came running.

Not recognizing Fiona's actions were intended to help the calf, the mama cow charged the woman and knocked her over. Try as she might, Fiona couldn't regain her footing before the cow charged again, this time putting its full weight on the woman.

By now, the woman, who was curled up in a ball with her arms wrapped around her head for protection, knew she was in a potentially deadly situation and was frantic to discover a way to make it back to safety when she heard another noise. This time, it was Kerry, the woman's 15-year-old chestnut mare that was quite literally kicking up a fuss, and the cow causing Fiona's panic was on the receiving end of that furor. While the horse was kicking the cow, Fiona managed to inch her way out of danger and crawl to safety.

Fiona later told reporters that she thought she was about to die that day. "I knew I had to get away from [the cow] or she was going to kill me, and as I tried to get up, the cow just fell right on top of me." Luckily, once Fiona called her husband, Matt, who'd been working in a neighboring field, and made her way to the hospital, it was discovered she suffered nothing more serious than a few cuts and bruises. Fiona readily admitted her horse was the reason she survived her ordeal.

While it's quite common to hear about how cats and dogs have rushed to the aid of their masters, one doesn't hear a lot about horses doing the same thing. It's certainly not unheard of, though. In 1978, a Morgan/Quarter horse named Indian Red, in Newmarket, Ontario, was inducted into the Purina Animal Hall of Fame for causing enough noise that someone eventually noticed the kerfuffle he was making and investigated the cause of the animal's anxiety. As it turned out, Indian Red had seen that a woman who'd been out walking on a wintery evening had fallen into a ditch full of snow. Had Indian Red not persisted in his efforts, the 77-year-old woman would quite likely not have survived the night.

All in a Day's Work

His neigh is like the bidding of a monarch, and his countenance enforces homage.

–William Shakespeare, writer

THE HALFINGER IS A BEAUTIFUL HORSE. Its coat, bordered by a blond mane, tail and socks, is the color and sheen of butterscotch. Measuring between 13.5 and 15 hands (4½ and 5 feet) and sturdy enough to carry a rider and pack, this breed is well equipped to work for its supper.

On April 23, 2007, 40-year-old Wolfgang Heinrich had a job in mind for his Halfinger, Sammy. After enjoying a romp through the countryside that lovely, spring evening, the German gentleman decided to meet a few of his buddies for a couple of brews at his local pub in the municipality of Wiesenburg/Mark, in the district of Potsdam-Mittelmark, Germany. Because he was on horseback, Heinrich didn't have to worry about drinking and driving—Sammy would get him home in one piece if he had too many beers.

Although he might not have planned to over-indulge, that's exactly what Heinrich did. It wasn't too long after he settled himself onto Sammy's back that he had second thoughts about continuing the journey. Sammy could certainly make it home in one piece, with or without Heinrich's guidance, but Heinrich couldn't guarantee he'd be able to stay in the saddle the entire way.

Faced with the prospect of spending a cold night outside if he didn't make it home, Heinrich came up with brilliant idea. Fumbling in his wallet, the man pulled out his bankcard and slid it through the card lock of a local bank. At the very least, the ATM booth would keep him warm for the night.

Of course, he couldn't leave Sammy outside on such a cold night. Besides, Heinrich didn't notice anywhere to tie Sammy up, and even if he did, someone could happen along and steal the horse. And so it was that Sammy also spent a warm night inside the bank. Heinrich stretched out, falling asleep as soon as his head hit the floor, and Sammy stood watch at the man's feet. Every so often, Sammy nudged his sleeping master with his muzzle, to make sure he was okay. Heinrich coughed, sputtered or mumbled a few words and then fell silent again. The entire night was recorded on the bank's video surveillance camera; Heinrich probably would have preferred rising before anyone noticed him there and forgetting the entire experience.

We all know that didn't happen, or else I wouldn't be telling you this story.

In fact, Heinrich didn't wake up until a few hours later when 36-year-old Stephan Hanelt happened along, looking to take a few dollars out of the ATM and finding a drunken man on the floor and a horse standing in his way! Hanelt placed one of the strangest calls ever taken by the local police department. Fortunately for Heinrich, he got off with nothing more than a stern reprimand and a warning not to use the bank to sleep off a night of drinking ever again.

Lucky for Heinrich, his horse was a hero as much for what he didn't do. Sammy didn't have a fit of rage at being locked in a small, strange place. The horse stood quietly and patiently waiting for his master to wake up. There were no hoof marks on the bank walls, and Sammy wasn't tempted to stomp on his master to teach him a lesson about drinking and riding his horse. Aside from having to relieve himself, Sammy managed to keep his head while his master had clearly lost his. The result was that Heinrich had nothing more to worry about the next day than a hangover.

For Sammy, it was all in a day's work.

Part Two

PETS WITH JOBS

Cats are smarter than dogs. You can't get eight cats to pull a sled through snow.

—Jeff Valdez, writer, comedian and producer

THE IDEA OF HARNESSING UP EIGHT, thick-coated, energetic huskies to pull a sled through a barren winter wasteland as a primary means of transportation has been around about as long as humankind has inhabited the cold, arctic regions of the North. It is an immensely beneficial partnership for the humans involved, who likely couldn't survive in these conditions without their canine chauffeurs, and the dogs thrive on the exercise and pretty much live for their jobs.

Single dog and handler teams also traverse the white wilderness, sometimes on crucial missions of mercy. The story of Balto, the Siberian husky who ran the anchor leg (53 miles) of a 674-mile journey hauling a diphtheria antitoxin from Nenana to Nome, Alaska, in an effort to eradicate an outbreak of the disease, is one example of the heroic capacity of this kind of working dog. Balto was one of the 20 dogs who spelled each other off throughout the journey, and their collective example is one of many stories of how a dog and a musher saved the day.

Of course, dogs work in many situations, not just as haulers. And although the quote at the beginning of this section is amusing, and there is some truth to it because cats don't haul their human friends around in sleds, don't be deceived into thinking that cats, and other animals, don't provide valuable and sometimes heroic services to us two-legged mammals. Read ahead and you'll see what I mean.

Dogs, Dogs, Dogs

If the work I make with my dog is shit, I am a shitty handler.

If the work is good, then it must be because of the dog.

—Author unknown

A Pit Bull that Made It Out of the Pits

People who treat other people [or other creatures] *as less than human* [or worthy] *must not be surprised when the bread they have cast on the waters comes floating back to them, poisoned.*

—James Baldwin, writer

IT'S DARK OUTSIDE, SAVE THE STARS cluttering the summer sky. The leaves flutter in the gentle breeze, and an occasional owl hoots for its mate. For most folks living in this rural location in Missouri, the evening promises a calm end to a busy day.

But there's a hum of anticipation building on a remote property tucked away in a corner of the state. Visitors are filing into the otherwise quiet country setting, arriving two or three at a time, keeping their voices low and proceeding with caution so they don't raise any unwanted attention. As they move ahead, they pass a crudely painted sign covering the side of a small building that warns, in blazing billboard fashion: "What you see here, hear here, stays here."

Sounds like Vegas but doesn't feel like Vegas. In fact, what's about to happen around the corner is not what most folks would consider Vegas-type fun, and yet it is, shockingly, considered enjoyment for some.

The roster for the night has been finalized. Bets placed. Everyone, with the exception of the "entertainment" that given the choice, would prefer to be anywhere else, was ready for the show to begin.

In the background, patrons hear the snarling and snapping of that evening's line-up. The dozen or more dogs biding their time before being thrust into the fighting ring are getting more anxious by the moment. They know what they are about to face.

It's kill or be killed.

It's incomprehensible to many of us that underground dog-fighting matches are big business throughout the United States and in many other countries, even though it's illegal. And yet a promising puppy from a proven prize-fighting lineage can fetch $5000, and there's enough of a market for this "sport" to make it profitable for the dog owners.

Tim Rickey, director of the Humane Society of Missouri's Animal Cruelty Task Force, had made it his personal quest to put an end to this kind of barbarism ever since he was called to a scene and found two dogs, one dead and bloodied and the other, the "winning" side of a dog-fighting match, very near death himself. Rickey has never managed to erase that image from his memory. It's what keeps him motivated.

Eradicating any form of savagery is an overwhelming task, but Rickey never let that distract him from what he needed to do. And on July 8, 2009, Rickey was on hand as some of his efforts bore tasty fruit indeed. He called it one of the best days of his life as, in a statement to the media, he outlined how "26 alleged dog fighters" in the eight states of Missouri, Illinois, Iowa, Texas, Oklahoma, Arkansas, Nebraska and Mississippi, had been arrested, and as many as "500 dogs were rescued." These dogs were transported to secret and secured rescue facilities in St. Louis.

The animals, emancipated from the hell they'd been born into and had lived in all their lives, were examined by veterinarians trained in animal rescue, and the condition of the dogs was nothing short of appalling. Because veterinarians don't jump at the opportunity to count owners and operators of dog-fighting rings among their clientele, the majority of the dogs suffered from any number of physical ailments. For some, deep wounds from previous fights were still raw and gaping. Many of the dogs were suffering from infections or worms and parasites or were hobbling on broken bones that hadn't healed. Most of the dogs' necks were blistered and chaffed. These injuries were caused by heavy, 30-pound chains tied to their thick collars: chains weighing as much as half the dog's weight were used to "strengthen" a dog's neck, an important quality in a prize fighter. At the same time, the chains rubbed against the dogs' thick, leather collars, skinning their necks bloody with the repeated movement. With a single, rare exception, all of the dogs were scared, unsure of what was about to occur.

Dogs that weren't deemed suitable for the fighting ring by the individuals running the events were used for one of two things: either they were breeders or they were bait. While life as a fighter was horrible, life as a bait dog was considerably more inhumane. Bait dogs were used to train young dogs to fight to kill, to build a sense of bloodlust in the fighters, and because these dogs didn't have it in them to protect themselves, they were terrorized until they finally died.

A fact sheet on dog fighting, produced by the Humane Society of the United States (HSUS), elaborates further on the conditions these dogs faced. The fights that the dogs (American pit bulls are a favorite breed for patrons of this "pastime") are forced into usually take place in walled pits and last an average of one to two hours. The fights most often conclude when one or the other dog is dead or quits fighting. To explain the kind of suffering involved, the HSUS quoted a description of dog-fighting brutality from *The Complete Gamedog*, a book written by American pit bull breeder and convicted dog fighter Ed Faron. The passage describes a fight between a dog named Bandit and another named Miss Rufus:

Miss Rufus spent most of the rest of the fight on her back and Bandit broke her other front leg high up in the shoulder, as well as one of her back legs, in the knee joint. The only leg she didn't break she chewed all to hell. She had literally scalped Miss Rufus, tearing a big chunk of skin off the top of her head alongside one ear.

It was this kind of horror that rescue workers uncovered in their search and seizure of eight properties. Seeing the brutalized animals they discovered must have broken the hearts of everyone involved in the recovery effort. But one dog in particular stood out among the rest. A dog that touched everyone she met. One dog that, despite all that she'd experienced, taught workers what it really meant to overcome adversity and not merely survive but thrive.

Looks Can Be Deceiving

From a distance, it was easy to believe that the five-year-old midnight-black pit bull chained to a wooden box on a rural Missouri property that July day in 2009 was baring her teeth and warning rescue workers to stay back. But Fay's tail, frantically whipping back and forth, faster and faster as workers got nearer, suggested joy and hopeful anticipation.

The seeming incongruity of this creature's behavior raised curiosity, but it wasn't long before the truth of her situation revealed itself. A closer inspection of the friendly female with the droopy eye brought the dog's real circumstances into horrifying clarity—she had no lips! Some stories about the rescue in general, and Fay in particular, initially suggested that the lips had been chewed or torn off in a dog fight while other stories speculated they were cut off to make her more deadly. In the end, it was determined that both were partial truths to her story. It was discovered that this once beautiful pit bull had her lips shredded in a fight, and then her owner cut off what was left—there was no way he'd have considered getting a veterinarian to fix the damage. The shocking reality that Fay had no lips solely because of the dog-fighting business soured the stomachs of those involved in the rescue even more. If they weren't overwhelmed with what they'd found to that point, Fay's reality certainly pushed everyone's tolerance level to the limit.

Abuse is a dangerous thing. Children who are abused and don't receive in-depth counseling to overcome the scars from living in that kind of environment are at risk for becoming abusers as adults. Animals are no different. In fact, they're often more doomed than their human counterparts. Traditionally, animals didn't always receive the kind of help and sensitivity available to people escaping these kinds of situations, and it is a commonly held belief that badly battered and abused dogs are irrevocably damaged—they could never be trusted again.

In the July raids, the Humane Society of Missouri (HSMO), the Humane Society of the United States (HSUS) and anyone involved with the HSUS 2010 Animal Survivor's campaign managed to rescue countless animals brutalized by human beings, but that was only half the battle. Now they had to prove that the dogs, which were not only bred for the fighting ring but were also what many individuals and governments typically consider "dangerous breeds," could be rehabilitated. These authorities had to inform public opinion about what was possible, given the right situation.

It wasn't long before those involved in the rescue effort, and the 2010 awareness and fundraising campaign, recognized that Fay, the tormented dog with no lips, held the key to winning over public support for this cause. Of course, the endeavor would require Fay to spend a lot of time in the public eye, attending HSUS events and meeting a curious public.

The HSUS couldn't have chosen a more fitting mascot.

Despite her years of mistreatment, Fay appeared to thrive on every chance at human interaction. She wagged her tail incessantly whenever someone looked her way. She'd just "melt into" a person's body when they stroked or held her, Fay's foster mom, Gale Frey, told reporter Amy Jamieson of *People Pets News,* referring to the first time Gale met Fay at the secure bunker where all the animals were first housed. Gale was volunteering there, and she noticed how Fay managed to win over the most hardened skeptic. There was no shortage of people willing to adopt the scared pup, but it was Gale who was lucky enough to receive the gentle creature at the St. Louis–based rescue group Mutts-n-Stuff. Gale and her husband, Dave Melot, founded the organization in 2000 after losing their Rottweiler to bone cancer. "I knew I wanted to take her [Fay] home to make a difference because she was a victim of dog fighting. And what the dog men did to her was just so cruel. I felt like we had to speak out. And I felt that she was the 'spokes dog' to do that."

Remarkably, her "toothy girl," as Gale took to calling Fay, continued to welcome familiar friends and strangers alike with the same enthusiasm throughout the weeks and months after her liberation from the fighting pit. Even during her rescue, while other dogs were leery of the volunteers and workers trying to assess their needs, Fay wagged her tail and greeted everyone with an unvarnished enthusiasm. She was the one dog that knew, inherently, that the people converging on the only home she'd ever known were there to help.

If anyone deserved a second chance at life it was Fay, and Gale did everything in her power to ensure that happened.

The Road to Rehabilitation

Socializing Fay obviously wasn't a huge concern. Aside from being spooked easily at sudden, loud noises, such as the sudden click of the spin cycle on a washing machine that would send Fay to the safety of her crate for days, it was hard to imagine the happy-go-lucky lady ever in the position where she would have had enough aggression in her to fight for her life. She was good with people of all ages;

children loved her, and her new mistress was obviously over-the-moon smitten.

To ensure that Fay had a good quality of life to look forward to, Gale needed to first address her physical problems. Fay's veterinarian, Dr. Marcy Hammerie, determined that the dog required reconstructive surgery to repair her damaged face. Dr. Hammerie consulted with plastic surgeons to assess the possibilities for success were she to reconstruct the dog's lips. This was important because, without her lips, Fay constantly drooled, and her gums dried out, causing her teeth and jawbone to degenerate. But before surgery could be done, Dr. Hammerie had to make sure there was adequate blood supply in the mouth area to support new tissue healing and growth. Fay also needed surgery on her nose: in her present condition, she could only breathe through her mouth, gurgling with each breath.

It would take three major surgeries and thousands of dollars to repair the damage Fay received at the hands of greedy people, but it was worth it to Gale. Donations came in to help pay for Fay's care as well—the HSUS reportedly provided $5000 toward Fay's medical expenses, and the veterinarians started preparing the dog for the work ahead and the healing process that would follow.

While Dr. Hammerie was ironing out Fay's physical rehabilitation, Gale was getting ready to enroll the dog in the American Kennel Club's Canine Good Citizen Program. Classes like this help dog owners spot any troublesome behaviors in their pets that they might not be objective enough to notice. This certification program would also give the pit bull a great foundation for future obedience classes and ensure both owner and dog have the basic skills required to move forward to other learning ventures. Gale was hoping that in time she could prepare Fay to become a therapy dog: Gale thought Fay would be a particularly inspiring visitor for veterans who'd lost limbs in combat.

"The veterans have gone through hard times during the war, and when they come back, they have to adjust to society," Gale told HSUS during an interview. "The same thing happens to fighting American pit bull terriers. They go from the fighting pits and then into society." Gale hoped Fay would provide veterans with the boost they needed to keep on going.

All in all, Fay's future was looking bright and hopeful.

Poster Pup for a Cause

While Gale's main concern was deciding on the best course of action for Fay's care, the American Society for the Prevention of Cruelty to Animals (ASPCA) was busy cataloging information on every dog apprehended, and collecting and documenting forensic evidence from the fight sites for use in court trials. By September, four members of the dog-fighting ring admitted their guilt in a St. Louis courtroom.

Of course, rehabilitating rescued animals and providing them with veterinary care, food and shelter, takes money—lots of money. It's a sad reality of the world we live in, but without the almighty dollar, a lot of things won't happen. Fay, easily interacting with others, and with her sparkling disposition despite the horrors she'd experienced, was a natural media darling. She became the poster child for the HSUS 2010 Animal Survivors Fund. Before Fay came along, the public might have been aware of the hundreds of dogs rescued in July, but now they had a face, and a personality, they could relate to.

A two-minute vignette designed as a public service announcement encouraging donations for the fundraising campaign outlined the repugnant situations faced by dogs born to a life of fighting. The public met Fay, watched her happily lick the face and hands of her caregivers, saw the soulful look in her eyes and heard testimony from workers involved in her care.

"This makes it worth the whole thing, I mean right here," one rescue worker shared on the video, stroking Fay's patchy coat and receiving all kinds of enthusiasm from the pup for his affection. "If it was only this one dog...all this work would be worth it."

As John Goodwin, HSUS spokesperson and one of the campaign organizers, explained: "Fay has suffered so much at the hands of human beings, she still demonstrated some faith in humanity."

This little dog, battered and beaten and brutally scarred, never let life beat her down. She wasn't just that poster child for animal rescue; she was an example of a creature with a passionate zest for life.

The Tide Changes

Fay's life was busy, full of activities, and she continued working for the cause. She never wanted for food or shelter, never went without her daily dose of love and cuddles, and at the same time she was also undergoing the succession of surgeries on her lips and muzzle. After the first operation, Dr. Hammerie had to make sure the sides of Fay's mouth healed properly before moving on to the reconstruction planned for her nose and upper lip.

The pit bull that survived hell and lived to inspire others continued to beat the odds. She recovered well from that first surgery, then the second, and her prognosis from the third surgery looked just as promising. On December 28, 2009, a few short moments after the last suture had been sewn on the third and final operation, Fay was beginning to wake from the anesthetic. Gale was a couple of feet from her side. Suddenly, it was all over. Fay's heart went into cardiac arrest. She died quickly and peacefully, the remnants of the anesthetic likely masking any pain she might have experienced. It was later determined her death was caused by "internal adhesions."

"In her previous life, she probably took some blows to the gut," Gale told reporters. "The scar tissue started twisting her intestines."

The media darling who touched the hearts of a nation was back in the spotlight, only this time her story broke hearts. No doubt anyone who had ever had the chance to meet and know her echoed the sentiments issued by the Humane Society of Missouri: "We are proud to have been able to rescue her and are grateful for every wet toothy kiss she shared with us since her rescue...we will miss her greatly!"

Fay continues to inspire change. Gale had already launched plans for the founding of Phoenix House, a type of "halfway home" for dog-fighting survivors to help them transition more smoothly into routine life. It was an initiative she'd hoped to share with Fay, and although the inspiration for Gale's idea is gone, the woman with a heart for needy animals will forge ahead in memory of the dog that stole her heart.

The 2010 Animal Survivors campaign also continues to use Fay as its mascot. And memories of the happy dog's toothy grin and sloppy kisses will continue to inspire rescue workers to excellence in their field.

In an Internet statement, Kristen Limbert, manager of field response for the ASPCA, had this to say: "Fay was a symbol of strength and resilience... But most importantly, she was an individual. An amazing dog who seemed to want nothing more than to move beyond her past and experience the kind of happy life she should have had all along."

Fay was a hero who inspired everyone she came into contact with during her lifetime. She continues to do so through her death.

To Serve and Protect: K-9 Heroes on the Job

One woman very courteously approached me in a grocery store, saying, "Excuse me, but I must ask why you've brought your dog into the store." I told her that Grace is a service dog... A few minutes later, she returned. "Excuse me, but you told me that your dog is allowed in the store because she's a service dog. Is she Army or Navy?"

–Terry Thistlewaite, British actor

AN OBSERVANT PERSON WITH A HEART for animals can easily recognize a dog's impact in any number of life situations. For example, a pup who is a well-loved and valued member of its family might, regardless of its training, rear up, bare its teeth and bark incessantly were it to sense any kind of threat being launched against its "people." Our furry friends know when we're sick or scared. They make us feel special with the frantic barks and wagging tails they show off in full Vegas splendor as soon as they hear the squeal of our car's brake pads, which lets them know we're finally home. Our dogs give us a sense of companionship and domestic bliss, and they'll protect us from any threat, real or imagined, with all their might. It only makes sense, then, that a dog's progression from hearth and home to the workforce, where they saddle up for a shift alongside their masters, wherever that might take them, would be a natural evolution.

But not everyone is a dog lover, and some battles for recognition have been hard-won victories.

Take the military, for example. Although forbidden in the trenches by most modern-day infantries until quite recently, the ancient Greeks and Egyptians took their canine companions into the theater of war as moral support, if for no other reason. That's probably how dogs made their way to the front lines of more recent armed conflicts. Having a dog with them was so important to some soldiers. They missed the sense of well-being and stability of home and were frightened about what their future might hold, so they often concealed dogs under their coats and packs and took them into the battlefields with them, despite the risk of serious reprimand from their superiors.

During World War I, the idea of animal companions entering the battleground at the front lines was becoming more and more common. It's not as if these soldiers intended Fido or Felix to protect them against the enemy, but that's often exactly what happened. Story after story emerged from the heat of combat. They told of how "war dogs," most of them mutts of uncertain lineage, rose to the occasion and not only supported troops with unconditional affection but also warned and protected soldiers from the threats of snipers, poisonous gas attacks and even the rats scuttling over their sleeping bodies. These stories produced a gem of an idea that could only blossom into something amazing.

Leading by Example

When the idea of admitting a dog to the front lines or using animals in police work was first raised, law enforcement and military officials routinely voiced their reservations about having dogs present in any sort of conflict situation. But the good press that dogs were getting from their war work couldn't help but leave folks scratching their heads in wonder. Stories emerged about dogs such as Rags, a shaggy, terrier-cross mutt who walked the fine line on his own or with his partner, Private James Donovan, and carried information from one unit to another under heavy fire.

Rags was responsible for delivering several crucial messages, and he survived the bombings, shootings and gasses of the war traveling to his destination. On more than one occasion his successful efforts were credited for saving a great many lives. On July 14, 1918, the U.S. 1st Infantry Division officially adopted the two-year-old pup as their mascot, and Rags continued to serve that unit until the end of World War I. Rags' partner, Donovan, on the other hand, died early on in the war, but by then, the dog had so captured the hearts of the other soldiers that he became a communal responsibility—everyone looked out for Rags, who lived to the ripe old age of 20.

There were many dogs like Rags serving in the trenches alongside their human partners. Some survived their war ordeals; others were not as lucky. In the United States, records on the influence of dogs on a soldier's life during early 20th-century conflicts, or the casualties those faithful servants might have experienced, weren't maintained until 1968. By the time the Vietnam War ended, the U.S. Army not only supported the use of dogs in war zones but also had started to track what was becoming a fairly substantial canine presence: one statistic suggested an estimated 5000 war dogs served in Vietnam between 1966 and 1973, and at least 43 of those four-legged soldiers died in the line of duty.

It was becoming increasingly clear that the animals that were at one time valued as simply loyal friends were also smart and willing helpmates in all types of situations. And if a dog could follow instructions and be a useful presence in the heat of armed conflict, it was a short leap to suggest that animals could serve equally well in civilian peacekeeping efforts. In fact, a dog's special skills, especially its keen sense of smell and fearless loyalty, could prove beneficial in a wide variety of regular police work.

The change of perception about how dogs and humans could work together was a gradual one, but change was on the horizon nonetheless.

First-of-a-Kind K-9

In the last 100 years or so, dogs have served as war dogs, ambulance dogs, naval dogs, search and rescue dogs and police dogs—in fact, they've performed just about any kind of service their human companions asked of them, and they've performed those duties to perfection. For the most part, meeting these demands came easy; a dog's loyalty to its master and its desire to please in every circumstance is such a strong motivator that it makes training a smart dog a fairly straightforward prospect.

Instructing dogs to assist in police work began more than 150 years ago. According to the Dumfries and Galloway Constabulary in the United Kingdom, the Belgian police force in Ghent was among the first in the world to regularly use dogs in their fight against crime. Some sources believe dogs were introduced to the Ghent police force as early as 1859; others suggest it didn't occur until the 1890s. In either case, these first working dogs were used to escort officers on night patrol, which made a lot of sense given that a dog's sense of smell and hearing is far more acute than that of humans, and those senses were endlessly beneficial in discerning threatening shadows lurking about during a night watch.

It appears that the Ghent experiment was a success because it wasn't long before the neighboring countries of Germany, France, Hungary and Austria took notice and began to develop a role for dogs in their police forces as well. However, constabularies in the United Kingdom remained a little more reserved about adopting the idea for their own officers; the Home Office didn't seriously analyze the topic until 1934. Even after an initial and in-depth study of the possibility of using dogs in this capacity, concerns surrounding potentially unpredictable behavior from a spooked or threatened animal stalled the process somewhat, and it wasn't until after World War II that dogs were first used to accompany police officers patrolling London's Hyde Park.

While exact numbers of dogs serving with police forces around the world aren't clear, today it's more the norm than the exception to find at least one K-9 officer assigned to most departments. They're used in routine patrols, to help in apprehending suspects, to sniff out drugs and bombs, and to attend to countless "high-risk" situations. These valuable animals continue to gain the respect of their human counterparts—when a police dog is killed in the line of duty, it is mourned by all.

A short poem penned by an unknown author offers a salute to police dogs that have died in the line of duty and are named on the Valour Row with the Canadian Police Canine Association:

The Working Dog
My eyes are your eyes,
to watch and protect you and yours.
My ears are your ears,
to hear and detect evil minds in the dark.
My nose is your nose,
to scent the invaders of your domain.
And so you may live,
my life is also yours.

The sentiment behind those few words will touch most with some kind of emotion. Read some of the stories behind those words, and you'll likely never look at a police dog the same way again.

Our K-9 Heroes

Tucked away in the heart of central Alberta is the community of Innisfail, home to 7883 residents, according to the town's 2009 census. Anthony Henday was the first European settler credited with passing through this prairie landscape in 1754. From the vantage point of a small rise on the landscape, not far from where the town now sits, Henday stood and gazed at the foothills of the Rocky Mountains to the west.

Originally named Poplar Grove by wagon and cart drivers traveling through the area, Innisfail got its name from the powers that be at the Canadian Pacific Railway (CPR) who eventually renamed the town based on a name of Celtic origin meaning "Isle of Destiny." The budding community certainly became an Isle of Destiny for the Danish and Icelandic settlers who, following Henday's footsteps some 100 years after he passed through, decided the place was too perfect to leave, and so they put down roots and established a town that is as unique as its name.

In 1965, the Royal Canadian Mounted Police (RCMP) searched out the best place to establish a dog training facility, and Innisfail was chosen. Some RCMP members had owned dogs prior to that time, but most of those early precursors to today's trained police dogs were personal pets with unique skills that assisted their masters in an unofficial capacity. In 1935, after noting the success stories behind some of these informal partnerships, the first "RCMP dog section" was formed. Black Lux, Dale of Cawsalta and Sultan were the first three German shepherds named to the dog team, and it was up to these brave forerunners to squelch any concerns surrounding the routine use of dogs in police work. Two years later, the dogs' hard work paid off, and the first official training school was established in Calgary, with the Innisfail facility founded two decades later.

According to its mission statement, the RCMP Police Dog Service Training Centre is a "national training centre established to provide suitable training and quality control in respect to all operational Police Service Dog (PSD) teams within the RCMP and those agencies who have requested and obtained training at the centre." It takes an investment of about $60,000 to train an RCMP dog team, but once that team is ready for action, the work they do is priceless. A good dog can search a vehicle in three minutes or less, sniffing for drugs, paraphernalia, weapons and even explosives.

More importantly, these dogs are trained to save lives.

PSD Cyr, Saskatoon Police Service

For the police, being called to a domestic situation is always unpredictable, especially when it escalates to crisis proportions. When police in Saskatoon,

Saskatchewan, arrived at Keldon McMillan's home on May 20, 2001, they were concerned about how they'd be received. McMillan's construction business had just gone bankrupt, he was wanted on firearms offences, and he was about to be served with an order preventing any contact with his estranged wife. As if that wasn't enough, McMillan allegedly told his wife that if the police were called into the situation, he would take his own life.

Clearly, McMillan was a man in crisis.

Police had every reason to worry. As McMillan drove near his home, he noticed the police were there and immediately tried to drive away. The police had anticipated his response and had blocked the roadway with unmarked cruisers. But that didn't deter McMillan—he drove across a lawn and raced onto a nearby highway, successfully avoiding the barricade and making his getaway.

The chase was on. Patrol cars tailed McMillan for almost 105 kilometers (65 miles) before a spike belt blew out the man's tires and he was forced to take off on foot.

Although McMillan no longer had wheels, he did have a gun, and he made sure to let police know it, firing two warning shots into the air. Desperate to get away, McMillan ran into a field and was moving toward a nearby farmhouse when Constable Steve Kaye, following close behind, led the chase and sent his canine partner Cyr ahead. It was crucial at this point to apprehend the suspect; everyone was concerned for the safety of residents should McMillan manage to take cover at the farmhouse.

McMillan knew the dog was rushing his way, and so the suspect raised his gun and fired two shots in Cyr's direction. Both hit Cyr, but he continued undaunted. Cyr then lunged for the man and grabbed hold before McMillan fired again. The third shot produced a fatal wound, and Cyr died at the scene in his handler's arms as Kaye's colleagues continued in the pursuit.

Still unwilling to back down, McMillan fired again, this time at the police officers. Police fired back, killing McMillan. The crisis was over, but the mourning had just begun. Kaye had lost his partner of three years, and the Saskatoon Police Department had lost a valued member. Cyr would also be missed by Saskatoon's school children who, over the years, had received regular visits from the police dog, proving he was not only a fighter but had a gentle and loving spirit as well.

More than 300 mourners attended Cyr's memorial service. One patron was so moved by the dog's ultimate sacrifice that he donated $10,000 to the Saskatoon Police Department so that bulletproof vests could be purchased for its dogs. The city named a park in Cyr's honor, and a youngster donated his puppy—Blue, a dog that happened to be Cyr's grandson—to Kaye. Although nothing could ever replace Cyr in anyone's hearts, perhaps Blue would prove a valuable addition to the police force and, in the process, make his famous granddad proud.

PSD Brix, Edmonton Police Service

Constable Gary Cook and his police dog Brix had been together since the pup was three months old. Those who knew Cook and his four-legged partner used to joke that you wouldn't find one without the other. Their unique bond carried over from their home life to the field. Cook was a veteran of the Edmonton Police Service, in Edmonton, Alberta, earning the respect of his peers through his years on the force, and it didn't take newcomer Brix long to follow in his master's footsteps. Aside from completing a 16-month training program to equip him to perform his duties, Brix earned Canadian Kennel Club titles in tracking and obedience, and the Schutzhund I (novice) title. "Schutzhund" is a German term meaning "protection dog," but the title is also given to dogs that excel in tracking and obedience. Between Cook's expertise and Brix's work ethic, the pair was destined to make an impression on their colleagues.

When it came to police work, Brix's classroom achievements and Cook's field experience blended together to create a productive team with countless successes. Police dogs such as Brix are fiercely protective of their handlers, but they're equally protective of the innocent victims they come across in the course of their duties. During one assignment, Cook and Brix were on the trail of a child abductor when the suspect panicked. Instead of dropping the three-month-old baby he'd been carrying, giving him a better chance at making a clean getaway, the perpetrator catapulted a dangerous situation into a potentially deadly one. Finding himself cornered and out of options for escape, the abductor faced off with the police and threatened the baby with a butcher knife. It was the partnership of Brix and Cook who successfully captured the man and ensured a safe close to a terrifying day.

For three years, Cook and Brix fought crime on Edmonton's city streets. Every day brought its fair share of challenges and successes. Like his master, Brix lived to capture criminals and restore a sense of peace in all manner of diverse situations. But on December 5, 1988, Brix's tenure with the force came to a sudden and sad end.

The partners were called to a scene where a group of males were reportedly checking out vehicles. In the midst of responding to the call, another patrol unit was trying to stop a suspicious vehicle that was driving at night with its lights off. When the driver of that vehicle wouldn't stop, the police picked up the pace and followed close behind until the vehicle crashed. The driver stumbled out of the car and quickly lost the police, who although they'd lost sight of the suspect, were still giving chase. By then, Cook and Brix were on the scene, and the dog had picked up the suspect's scent. In his desire to catch his prey, Brix set off after the individual at full speed.

We all know how quickly things can happen. This routine apprehension should have ended as successfully as the many others that had preceded it. But Brix, in his single-minded focus on cornering the suspect, rushed across the road into the path of an oncoming police cruiser. The brave dog that had earned the moniker "big guy" and had a reputation as a tireless worker was hit by the car. The force of the impact propelled the pup into the air. He fell at his master's feet. Brix died in Cook's arms.

Brix was Edmonton's first Police Service Dog to die in action. As devastating as the dog's death was to Cook and other members of the police force, Cook recognized the significance of his partner's death, saying, "He died doing what he loved to do...pursuing the 'bad guys.'"

PSD Chip, Hope, British Columbia

Constable Doug Lewis had been with the RCMP for 18 years. The skilled and dedicated officer had a long list of joys and sorrows he'd witnessed during his tenure, but one of the most gratifying experiences he'd had was his work as a canine handler. By the time he and Chip, his canine partner at the time, responded to a call on September 13, 1996, to assist police in tracking a suspect who'd fled into the woods near Hope, British Columbia, Lewis had been working as a handler for seven years.

Lewis and Chip weren't officially on duty at the time, and the officer didn't have his gun, handcuffs or other equipment with him, but the Emergency Response Team (ERT) requesting his help assured Lewis that all he and Chip needed to do was locate the suspect. Any kind of direct contact would come from the ERT members already at the scene.

The suspect, who didn't appear to be armed, was a large man described as more than six feet tall and weighing around 235 pounds. He had been aggressive and defiant, resisting arrest and fleeing the officers who'd pulled him over for leaving a gas station without paying and running a tollbooth near the town of Merritt, BC. It seemed to be a fairly straightforward tracking assignment, and so Lewis and Chip drove the 30 minutes or so from Chilliwack to Hope.

Once at the scene, Chip and Lewis got to work. The dog picked up the suspect's scent right away and tracked him almost two miles up the mountainside and into the woods before the team came face to face with its man. On Lewis' command, Chip charged the suspect, latching on to the man's arm.

Nobody was prepared for what came next.

In his free hand, the man was holding a knife. He started slashing at Chip, plunging the weapon into Chip's neck and piercing his jugular vein. Lewis rushed at the man in an earnest attempt to protect Chip. That's when the man turned on Lewis and began slashing at the officer. Although Chip could barely walk, the dog garnered enough energy to lash out at the deranged man once more, biting and attacking him enough that in the confusion, Lewis was able to knock the knife out of the man's hand.

Rushing for help, and bleeding heavily in the process, Lewis managed to retrace his steps to find the ERT personnel still making their way to the scene. It took five hours, a bevy of 30 officers, seven canine units and a police helicopter to finally apprehend the suspect.

Meanwhile, Lewis was rushed to hospital with nine stab wounds to his face and upper body. It took 50 stitches to sew him up. Chip wasn't so lucky. The faithful dog died at the scene.

It took some time before Lewis felt comfortable getting another dog. Chip's memory, and the events of that otherwise lovely fall day, remained fresh and vivid years later, and the grief Lewis feels over the loss of Chip will always be there.

It's been said that the best revenge is living well. Instead of giving in to his grief, Lewis continued to work with dogs and teach other officers about issues of safety. He encourages everyone he comes into contact with by his positive outlook on life. And if there's one thing Chip and the confrontation in the woods taught Lewis, it's that you should never give up.

PSD Sirk, Calgary Police Service

We've all heard people voice their concerns about the ins and outs of law enforcement, and how criminals would think twice about breaking the law if certain outspoken individuals were in charge. But there's a reason why vigilante behavior is frowned upon—more often than not, taking the law into one's own hands is dangerous and sometimes deadly.

For three years, Constable Garth Blais and Sirk, a German shepherd born and trained in Germany before coming to Canada in 1986, had worked together with the Calgary Police Service. Blais was no stranger to working with police dogs. Prior to and during his three years of working with Sirk, the constable had another canine partner, a dog named Chance that specialized in sniffing out drugs. The trio often worked together on a variety of assignments, but it was Sirk who was often seen as a "star" in the CPS. Sirk could be single-minded in his goals; Blais reported that the dog could "rip a wall apart to get to the drug on the other side." At the same time, Sirk knew how to be soft and gentle when necessary, like the time he and Blais found a 2½-year-old child who'd wandered off into a field. "When [Sirk] found him, he was just like a puppy—so gentle," Blais told officials from the Canadian Police Canine Association.

As a team, Sirk and Blais had gone through all kinds of situations together. Shortly after the two teamed up, Sirk broke three of his legs trying to chase down a robbery suspect. Aside from a noticeable limp, Sirk didn't slow down much. Once his wounds had healed, he was back in the field, chasing down suspects and backing up Blais, which, as it turned out, was fortunate for Blais.

In the summer of 1989, the good constable found himself up against an angry suspect pointing a shotgun in his direction. Unable to apprehend the would-be shooter or talk the suspect down from his emotionally charged state, Blais would have found himself seriously, if not fatally, injured had it not been for Sirk's quick reflexes. As the agitated gunman pulled the trigger, Sirk lunged in his direction, successfully deflecting the weapon, which discharged into the air, missing Blais and anyone else in the area. Blais survived the ordeal, and the gunman was apprehended.

That kind of loyalty produces a bond that only death can break.

On the night of December 13, 1989, Blais stepped away from his police cruiser for a short time and when he returned, he found Sirk convulsing and struggling to breathe. Blais drove immediately to the veterinary clinic, but Sirk died on the way. While Blais was shocked at his sudden loss, he was more surprised by the postmortem findings. It appeared that Sirk died as a result of strychnine poisoning. An investigation examined every scenario that could have led to Sirk coming across the deadly substance. It was eventually discovered that a man named Mario Gaudin had added the poison into a bran mixture to kill what he'd considered to be pesky squirrels in the area. In his single-minded, rather violent approach to dealing with his "problem," Gaudin's poisoned mixture managed to kill six dogs. Sirk, who had responded to a call in that area that night, was the last dog to die. In October 1990, the 62-year-old Gaudin was found guilty of poisoning all six dogs. The City of Calgary followed up with a civil suit of its own, suing the man for $50,000—the approximate cost of replacing Sirk.

The money might have bought another dog—one that would have been cherished as much as Sirk had been—but it could never replace Blais' lost partner.

PSD Nitro, Vancouver Police Department

Any parent will tell you that if you want to instill a sense of loyalty in an older child when a new addition to the family is introduced, it's probably wise to include that youngster in caring for the newcomer. Perhaps it was that kind of philosophy that led the Vancouver Police Department to hold its first ever "Name the Puppy" contest for the newest puppy to be assigned to its force. Regardless the motivation, the newcomer, named Nitro by Vancouver's school children, quickly captured the hearts of an entire city.

Nitro was two years old when the sable-haired shepherd with the soulful eyes completed his training and was paired with Constable Howard Rutter in 1999. Affections ran deep between the seasoned officer and his canine partner, and their partnership was so successful that they were nominated for the Vancouver Police Department's Police Officer of the Year Award. Despite Nitro's smaller-than-normal size for a dog chosen to serve on the K-9 unit, he was recognized as one of the most productive police dogs in the force. Nitro's many success stories included rounding up a dangerous suspect in a sexual assault and stabbing case in 2002 and tracking down an armed robber in 2003, to name just two.

By January 2006, the noble shepherd developed arthritis and was to retire that coming April. Having lived with Constable Rutter and his family since 1999, Nitro was set to spend his remaining years in their loving home. But it was only January, and he hadn't yet retired.

At about 10:30 on the night of January 23, Nitro and Rutter were taking part in a dog-and-handler training class when an officer in an unmarked police cruiser noticed a stolen car on Marine Drive and Argyle. Rutter and his partner were called to help in pursuit of two suspects, and the chase led them into New Westminster and to a train crossing on Front Street.

What happened next was witnessed by several police officers, volunteers working with the dog training team and Constable Rutter. Faced with the inability to continue by car because a train blocked the roadway, the two occupants in the stolen vehicle bolted on foot. Nitro, focused on apprehending at least one of the men, leapt after the pair, latching on to one of the men as he tried to jump on the train, which by that time had slowed down to little more than a crawl. Nitro looked like he'd caught the suspect by the leg, but as the train started gaining speed, the ebb and flow of tension caused the cars to lunge and clank. The jarring movements caused a staccato motion and Nitro lost his grip on the suspect. The dog fell to the tracks and was killed by the rolling train.

Nitro's injuries were "very, very traumatic…it was horrible," Sergeant Gord Park, head of Vancouver's canine unit, told *The Vancouver Province*. "I would think he was killed instantly."

Nitro was the eighth canine member of the Vancouver Police Department killed in the line of duty. His tenure with the force garnered him so much respect that 400 officers from across Canada and the United States attended an open memorial in his honor on February 6, 2006. As for the public connection that began with a simple contest urging school children to come up with a name for Vancouver's newest police puppy, it grew exponentially. And on the day of Nitro's memorial service, hundreds of civilians came to say thank you and to bid farewell to a dog that gave his life to help keep city streets safe.

Nitro's working days aren't over, however. In keeping with that city's tradition, the dog's ashes were scattered around city limits where it's believed the dog's spirit will continue to keep watch over the residents of Vancouver and protect them for all time.

PSD Bandit, Cape Breton, Nova Scotia

Sources aren't clear on what upset 22-year-old Ian Matthew MacDonald on the morning of

June 25, 2000, but the man was dangerously troubled. Police who'd been called to MacDonald's home had been trying to calm him for hours, but the man kept pacing around the yard and threatening to kill anyone who came too close.

The Emergency Response Team (ERT) had yet to arrive at the scene when MacDonald decided to take a walk. Leaving his yard, and following the railway tracks near his home, MacDonald made his way toward a local store. Concerned that the situation could intensify and involve other innocent people should MacDonald enter the store, some of the officers at the scene moved to block the man's path.

Recognizing their intentions, MacDonald retreated to the safety of his home. What MacDonald didn't realize was that Corporal Rick Mosher and his dog, Bandit, had taken up position between MacDonald and his house, blocking the man's path. As MacDonald moved closer to his home, Bandit and Mosher prepared to intercept him. When he saw his chance, Bandit rushed MacDonald, grabbing him by the arm and holding firm. For a while, the two played an angry tug-of-war with Bandit pulling MacDonald around in circles. MacDonald, who unbeknownst to officers was armed with a knife, started slashing at Bandit. It was clear to Mosher, who was nearby, that MacDonald had connected at least once with the police dog, but Bandit didn't back down. Recognizing the danger, Bandit was not only focused on apprehending the suspect but was also determined to protect Mosher.

Mosher, on the other hand, was anxious to protect Bandit from serious injury. He called Bandit away from the suspect, drew his weapon and fired two warning shots, trying to deter an angry MacDonald from coming any closer. At the same time, neither Mosher nor Bandit wanted to give up on their pursuit altogether. Once again Bandit leapt onto MacDonald just as the man plunged the knife into the animal. Mosher fired his gun again, this time wounding MacDonald. The suspect was finally apprehended, but by then Bandit was silent, bleeding heavily and lying in a heap on the ground. The dedicated police dog died at the scene.

The altercation that cost Mosher his partner must have been a harrowing one at the time, but the depth of Bandit's dedication wasn't fully revealed until a postmortem on the dog was conducted. In the midst of MacDonald's frantic slashing, he'd connected with Bandit more severely than anyone could have guessed judging by the dog's reaction. It appeared that at one point during the battle, Bandit's spinal cord had been partially severed, and yet the dog never gave up until he couldn't give anymore.

Losing Bandit was devastating for Mosher. "When he was killed, I lost a piece of me," the corporal told the Canadian Police Canine Association.

Bandit was posthumously inducted into the Purina Hall of Fame as the Service Dog of the Year in 2001 for his valiant efforts.

His attacker walked away with little more than a slap on the wrist. At the suspect's trial, Mosher testified that he believed his dog prevented innocent people from being harmed—he was hoping to win some recognition in the courts about the devastation MacDonald caused, but the man's lawyers argued that, "a police dog is nothing more than a tool and that this kind of outcome was to be expected in the line of duty."

While it appears clear that law enforcement personnel have accepted dogs in the field and value their contribution in the fight against crime, at the time of this writing, Canada still has not established a law against killing a police service dog. In the United States, laws against that kind of offense vary from state to state. In February 2010, South Dakota passed a bill making the killing of a police dog a "Class 6 felony" and any action to intentionally injure this animal in any way a "Class 1 misdemeanor." The bill has yet to proceed to the Senate. But in the states of California, Indiana, Iowa, Massachusetts, New Jersey, Ohio, Oregon, Texas and Utah, there are statues on the books that protect police service dogs. Similar laws are being proposed in other states as well.

K-9 Sevo, Topeka, Kansas

The life of a K-9 officer is typically centered on confrontation. So when Officer Scott Gilchrist and his K-9 partner Sevo responded to a request to assist another officer, it was just another day on the job for the pair.

Of course, when it comes to law enforcement, there's never any such thing as "just another day on the job."

On that lovely fall day, September 23, 1998, when the leaves were turning gold and most folks were already beginning to plan ahead to Thanksgiving and Christmas, Gilchrist and Sevo were focused on tracking down a suspect. The pair was responding to a disturbance call when Gilchrist spotted the suspect, who by then had fled the scene on foot. Gilchrist identified himself as a police officer and ordered the suspect to stop.

Of course, if everyone listened to a police officer when ordered to halt, we'd be living in a far more orderly world. The suspect, noticing Gilchrist closing in on him, turned and ran in the opposite direction.

Gilchrist called him down again. This time the suspect appeared to be grabbing something from the area of his waistband. Preparing for the worst, Gilchrist drew his gun and again ordered the suspect to stop.

The suspect turned and faced Gilchrist and, armed with a knife, charged toward Gilchrist and Sevo who, until that moment, had been in the heel position.

Making repeated slashing motions with his knife, the individual continued to rush toward Gilchrist and his dog. With his gun focused on the suspect, Gilchrist ordered Sevo to apprehend the man.

By then, Sevo could sense the suspect's anxiety and potential threat to his handler and was more than ready to attack. Sevo latched onto the suspect's arm, but the man didn't appear fazed by the attack. Instead, with his knife at the ready, the perpetrator began slashing and stabbing Sevo as he continued to make his way toward Gilchrist.

Realizing the man wasn't about to back down, Gilchrist fired his weapon twice. The suspect shouted out that he'd been hit but continued to slash his knife and stumble toward Gilchrist. Gilchrist fired twice more before the man finally halted his attack and was safely taken into custody.

Sevo, however, had been badly injured in the attack. Veterinarians did all they could to help the police dog, and Sevo rallied for some time. But on December 31, 1998, he finally succumbed to his injuries. Sevo is only one of several K-9 officers to be killed in the line of duty, and he was honored for his ultimate sacrifice by the North American Police Work Dog Association.

K-9 DiOGi, Polk County, Florida

Some people just seem destined to fulfill a certain role in life from the time of their birth. Deputy Sheriff Matt Williams was one of those people. The 12-year veteran of the Polk County Sheriff's Office was proud of his badge and his track record as a dedicated and reliable officer. He was also proud of his title as the head trainer of the county's K-9 Unit. For the last eight years of his tenure, Williams had worked with his own police dog, his most recent acquisition being DiOGi or, as he liked to joke, "the DOG with two li'l i's."

Working with a police dog had infused Williams' career with new energy, and the typically upbeat officer was always eager to share new ideas on how to work with a K-9 partner. Those who ever met Williams remember him saying, "As long as I get up in the morning and I see my patrol car still says 'CAUTION K9,' I know it's going to be a good day."

Regardless of the stressors Williams faced at any given time, every day was a good day as far as he was concerned.

Just before noon, on September 28, 2006, Williams and DiOGi were responding to a call to assist another officer near 10th Street and Wabash in Lakeland. Deputy Douglas Speirs had been following a suspect who had ditched his vehicle and rushed into a wooded area near that intersection. Williams and DiOGi tracked the suspect and cornered him near a downed tree.

The officers didn't know the suspect was in possession of a loaded gun until he fired at and hit DiOGi just as the dog leapt at the man. Before Williams had the chance to return fire, the suspect started shooting at the officer, hitting him eight times before stopping and retrieving Williams' police gun and ammunition and rushing behind a nearby house.

By now, several SWAT and K-9 teams from all corners of Polk County descended on the scene with two goals: finding out what happened to Williams and DiOGi and apprehending the dangerous suspect. In a game of cat and mouse, law enforcement personnel tracked the man's movements for nearly 24 hours when finally, at 9:50 the following morning, they could see the suspect huddled underneath a fallen tree. At that point, as many as 500 officers were involved in the manhunt, but the man still refused to surrender. When he raised Williams' service revolver, threatening the officers before him, he was shot dead.

Sadly, Williams and DiOGi both died from their gunshot wounds. Their heroic efforts have been memorialized throughout Polk County. Now, when officers think of the fallen team, they remember Williams as "the exemplary Handler we shall strive to be" and "DiOGi [as] the K-9 partner we will compare our own to."

K-9 Koda, Midvale, Utah

Sometimes an animal portrays a powerful and lasting impression, even when the animal has been known only for a short time.

Such was the case with K-9 officer Koda.

The three-and-a-half-year-old Belgian Malinois police dog had only worked with the Midvale Police Department for 18 months, but in that brief time, he'd forged a special bond with anyone who came into contact with him. With a persistently wagging tale and energetic disposition, Koda was more like a big puppy than a responsible, working adult dog. But looks can be deceiving, and when it came to doing his job, Koda was all business.

Officer Brian Todd and his partner Koda had been called to a burglary complaint around 8:30 on the evening of Friday, January 1, 2010. When the team and other police officers arrived at the home, they discovered three men and a woman trying to escape in a car. But the roads were icy, and the occupants in the car appeared to think they'd have a better chance eluding police with the divide-and-conquer approach and took off on foot. Officers quickly captured 33-year-old Clinton Sean Peterson, who appeared to be "heavily intoxicated" at the time, but the other three suspects were a little harder to apprehend.

As the story unfolded, and the officers learned a little more about the individuals they were dealing with, it became increasingly clear that there was potential for a violent altercation. Police knew each of the men because some of them were facing charges for everything from burglary to possession of stolen vehicles.

While one of the men fled into the home, locking himself inside, 22-year-old Tevita Talanoa Fisiitalia ran into a neighbor's backyard. Todd and Cottonwood Heights officer Chris McHugh followed close behind

Fisiitalia, led by Koda. The dog rushed Fisiitalia, grabbing the man by the forearm as Fisiitalia fired two shots into the dog. The suspect continued to run, his 9-mm handgun still in plain sight. Todd returned fire, shooting Fisiitalia in the head. The man later died in hospital.

Koda's injuries were also fatal, and there was no doubt among the officers at the scene that had the dog not reacted with such precision, one of them might have received a fatal gunshot wound.

"Officers were in jeopardy from the moment they arrived that night," Midvale Captain Steve Shreeve told the more than 1000 mourners gathered for Koda's memorial service. "[Koda] gave his life so others would not have to. He did what he was trained to do."

It was a sentiment echoed in several media reports about the incident. "He did his job, and he did it well," Midvale Police Sergeant Marcelo Rapela told Wendy Leonard of the *Deseret Morning News*. "He may have saved the life of one or more of our officers." The officers who worked with Koda, as well as colleagues from other states, gathered to acknowledge the K-9's value to law enforcement in Midvale. Members of the public flooded the memorial service, and Platt Electric Supply, a local company headquartered in Oregon, donated $4000 and a private plane in order for the Midvale police to purchase and retrieve Koda's replacement. Thanks to that donation, Kuno arrived and was ready to be initiated into the department a week after Koda's death.

While Koda will never be forgotten, Kuno came ready to take up the challenge and carry on where his predecessor left off.

To ensure no one forgets the ultimate sacrifice Utah's K-9 officers have made throughout the years, the Utah Police Service Dog Memorial is being built at the Utah Peace Officer Standards and Training campus in Sandy.

K-9 Bandit, Sacramento, California

Home invasions are sudden, terrifying and unpredictable. Most times, homeowners don't know the person barging into their house, and the intense aggression displayed by that kind of brazen action clearly suggests the possibility for extreme violence.

At around 8:35 on the evening of March 16, 2010, a 17-year-old babysitter and the five-year-old boy she was caring for were preparing for a peaceful evening when 32-year-old Meng Xiong allegedly barged into the house on the 2000 block of O'Neil Way. One of the occupants of the house managed to call 9-1-1, but the man, who appeared intent on robbing the home, grabbed the two youths and tied them up. The suspect was still inside when police arrived and surrounded the house.

Panicked, the would-be robber tried to escape through the back of the house where Officer Gary Dahl and his K-9 partner Bandit were stationed. Bandit charged the robber in an effort to take him down, but the dog was shot in the altercation.

The robber disappeared back into the house and then out the front door. Refusing to drop his weapon, and in the course of threatening police, the suspect was shot and killed. Police later discovered the man was allegedly communicating by telephone with his 23-year-old brother, Zang, during the robbery. Zang was apprehended and arrested later that same day as an accomplice.

Thankfully, the two children involved in the horrifying event weren't physically injured. The same couldn't be said for Bandit, though. The dog was rushed to the VCA animal hospital and prepped for immediate surgery. It took five hours to patch Bandit up; the bullet that hit Bandit entered the left side of his neck and embedded itself on the right side. Although an injury like that could have done a lot of damage, Bandit was lucky. "Somehow it missed everything," Officer Dahl's wife, Lynette, told reporters from KXTV. "It's a miracle. He's lucky to be alive."

The slug and bullet fragments were successfully removed from Bandit's neck, and although Bandit needed a good deal of time to recover, at least this potentially deadly situation ended happily.

Remembering Our K-9 Heroes

These stories are just a sampling of the heroic sacrifices made by police dogs over the last century. Canada's law enforcement dogs that have died in the line of duty are commemorated on the National Police Dog Monument at the Royal Canadian

Mounted Police K-9 Training Centre in Innisfail, Alberta. The Animals in War memorial recognizes all kinds of animals used in times of conflict. Princess Anne unveiled the monument in November 2004 in London's Hyde Park. Australia also recognizes its war dogs in an official memorial in Goolwa, Australia, and a similar monument was erected in honor of Guam K-9s who died in 1944.

The work of police dogs and dogs who served in war, whether they did so officially or not, is also recognized across the United States. Utah is looking at building a memorial for its fallen K-9 officers. In 2009 alone, several police dog memorials were unveiled: the Virginia Law Enforcement K-9 Memorial on October 16, the Stanislaus County Sheriff's Department K9 Memorial was dedicated on October 2, the Pineville Kentucky K-9 Memorial was unveiled on September 28, and the Miami Police K-9 Memorial was completed on May 1.

A memorial located at J.P. Case Middle School in Flemington, New Jersey, recognizes Vietnam's many war dogs. The Vietnam K-9 and Dog Handler Memorial was officially dedicated on May 18, 2009.

Countless individual memorials honoring specific K-9 officers and their handlers have also been built in communities around the United States. Among the most touching of those memorials is the one that honors officer Matt Williams and his partner DiOGi, who died together doing the job they both loved.

The team of Williams and DiOGi is recognized by Polk City, Florida, as "Our Hometown Heroes."

While a few skeptics might doubt the validity of the kind of work a police dog does during its tenure, or think a dog is like any other "piece of equipment" and therefore its death in the line of duty is nothing more than collateral damage, it's clear that most folks think otherwise.

They see them as heroes.

Snake Dogs Never Back Down

The nose of the bulldog has been slanted backwards so that he can breathe without letting go.

–Winston Churchill, British prime minister

DEPENDING ON WHERE YOU LIVE, the frequency of interactions between dogs and snakes varies, and the concerns surrounding those interactions are quite different. In the Canadian prairies, the worst that could happen to your dog if it came up against a feisty garter snake is getting nipped. Considering that garter snakes aren't poisonous and are quite small and unable to inflict much more than a slight nick on the dog's skin should it manage to penetrate the canine's coat, the run-in would turn out to be little more than a bothersome nuisance.

However, in the wilds of Ontario, dogs have a far larger variety of snakes to contend with. There are 17 species of snakes in this eastern Canadian province. Some, such as the black ratsnake, can grow as long as nine feet and give your pet quite a fight should it get entangled with one of these specimens. The Eastern Massassuaga, Ontario's only venomous snake species, could conceivably cause some damage to your pup. And I'd venture to guess that most of us wouldn't want our pet pooch to come home with this kind of treasure wrapped around its neck—although in certain parts of the world, the idea of Fido coming home with a snake necklace isn't unheard of.

In some countries, encounters between pets and snakes can be far more frequent—and deadly. In Australia, where snakes are plentiful and many are of the poisonous variety, a "lights out" check through the house in rural areas likely includes a quick peek under the furniture for any wayward serpents that might have snuck in unnoticed during a busy day. In that country, families with dogs are often warned when one of the many varieties of snakes makes its way near a home. Their dog's unique alarm system, which often entails frantic running around in circles and incessant barking at something in the grass at their feet, alerts families that a snake is nearby. In light of some of these snakes' venomous qualities, it's a good thing the family pet is instantly repelled by these wild varmints. Should a large dog get nipped by a tiger snake, for example, it might end up at the animal hospital for a few days, but it would probably survive. The same might not be true for a small child who is bitten by this potentially deadly creature.

Although animal experts advise dog owners to teach their pets to stay away from snakes and to protect them from any unnecessary exposure to the reptiles, in some cases this isn't possible. Certain dogs are driven to chase and kill unwanted snakes, and in some situations that instinct has saved lives.

Talk About Smart

One story from Down Under involves Bronson, an 11-year-old black Labrador retriever that was unfortunate enough to come into contact with a deadly copperhead. This snake loves grassy areas and woodlands, so it's quite possible Bronson happened upon the creature in the family's back yard, which this slithering chunk-head likely thought was a lovely, grassy haven.

In January 2010, the well-trained hunter with a strong inclination toward self-preservation was quick enough to snap at the copperhead as it lunged toward him in an attempt to sink its fangs into the dog's flesh. Bronson connected with his attacker, all right. However, he ended up in a considerable dilemma. With his mouth closed around the reptile, Bronson was seemingly aware that he hadn't killed the creature, which meant that the dog was in a difficult, if not impossible, situation.

Not wanting to risk a potentially deadly bite, Bronson kept his mouth shut and made his way back home. On noticing Bronson arrive at the back door looking quite concerned, and with something hanging from his mouth, his owners Deborah and Peter Allen went out to investigate. They saw that the snake had wrapped its body around Bronson's nose.

Thankfully, Bronson behaved like the brilliant hunting dog he was, keeping his mouth firmly shut around his prey until his owners gave him the appropriate order. According to an article in the *Herald Sun*, Deborah placed a cloth bag around the bottom of the snake's body, teasing it to release its grip around Bronson's nose. Bronson, meanwhile, didn't move a muscle until Deborah gave the order.

"Give!" Deborah shouted.

Bronson dropped his prey into the bag and his mistress snapped the bag shut.

Because the snake had bitten Bronson, the dog required a visit to the veterinary hospital and an intravenous drip to administer the antivenin. But he survived his ordeal. He was, in effect, his own hero!

Quick Reflexes

A little closer to home, a 13-year-old Danville, Virginia, youngster was planning to enjoy his first church mission trip of sorts in June 2008. Haiasi Sampson was helping about 20 other members of his church lead a Vacation Bible School in neighboring Kentucky when the unthinkable happened.

The young member of the Episcopal Church of the Epiphany was hauling dirt in a wheelbarrow when he nearly rolled over a three-foot copperhead snake.

Noticing the snake coiled in front of him, Sampson froze. The snake had clearly seen the boy nearby and must have felt threatened, as it was coiled and preparing to strike when a small, homeless beagle-cross that had taken a liking to the teen intervened. The pup barked at the reptile at the same time that the snake struck out at the young Sampson, missing his face by mere inches. The dog's barking diverted the snake's attention, and so the beagle became the subject of the reptile's wrath.

Once bitten, the beagle stumbled, then fell over. Confident in its victory, the snake slithered away. Sampson breathed a quick sigh of relief over his own good fortune, but his joy was short-lived. Rushing over to the pup's side, it was clear to Sampson that the young beagle was severely injured. Sampson's pastor, the Reverend Sam Colley-Toothaker, took the dog to the veterinary hospital, and his quick intervention was instrumental in saving the small dog's life. Sampson named the beagle "Sparky" because it moved so quickly, and he told reporters from the *Danville Register & Bee* that he believed God sent the dog to save him.

While it's not uncommon for an animal to risk life and limb to protect his master, this pup risked all to protect a virtual stranger.

Now that's what I call a hero.

Rattlesnake Wranglers

A dedicated dog owner living in rattlesnake country would be wise to protect his pooch from a potential interaction with a rattler. That said, some dogs seem destined to tangle with the venomous snake no matter how loud it rattles its warning or how hard the dogs' owners work at training their pet to stay away. Instead of repelling the canine attacker, the sound of a rattle raises ire in the dog that it simply can't suppress. In short order, a standoff occurs, with the snake aggressively defending itself. A born "snake dog," as they're often called by the folks familiar with this seemingly innate tendency in their pets, is fearless, lightning fast and fights to the finish regardless how many times it has been bitten in the process. It's a dangerous obsession—one that can cost a dog its life. But there are many situations where this kind of tendency is more than just welcome; it's a lifesaver.

A bite from the more venomous varieties of rattlesnake can have deadly results, especially when untreated. As many as 8000 rattlesnake bites are reported in the United States every year; an average of five of those victims succumb to their injuries. Others inflicted with a bite could experience a wide range of symptoms, from difficulty breathing and loss of motor control to more severe reactions such as shock or internal hemorrhaging.

Children are especially vulnerable to the poison injected through the fangs of one of these deadly vipers. Their much smaller bodies have a far more difficult time combating the poison, and even though they might survive a bite, they could suffer from lingering and lifelong difficulties. So if you're a parent and happen to live in an area where rattlers roam, having a protective dog with a penchant for chasing away unwanted pests doesn't feel like such a bad thing.

On May 29, 2009, seven-year-old Gaven Welch was near the backyard fence of the home where he and his mother live near Box Springs Mountain in California's Moreno Valley when the precocious youngster spotted what he recognized as a red diamondback rattlesnake nestled amid a pile of rocks. The snake hissed at the boy. Gaven knew this wasn't a good thing, especially when he noticed the snake was three or four feet long. Despite the danger, he found himself unable to move.

Nikita, a five-year-old Japanese Akita belonging to Tammy and Todd Halderman, the couple renting a room to Gaven and his mother, didn't hesitate for a second. The quick-thinking dog, apparently well versed in this kind of scenario, barked and lunged at the rattler, shocking Gaven out of his stupor long enough for the boy to turn and run to the safety of the house. Gaven knew he had walked away unscathed because of Nikita's loyalty and determination, but the dog was still out there, and before a neighbor managed to intervene and shoot the snake, Nikita was bitten three times on her face.

Because the dog was transported to an animal hospital almost immediately after receiving the bites, she managed to survive her injuries. The episode reinforced for Gaven the desire to stay indoors. At the very least, when he does venture outside again, he told *The Press-Enterprise*, he plans on making sure Nikita is with him.

Kay Harrison of Tonopah, Arizona, likely feels much the same.

In April 2010, Kay Harrison was enjoying a relaxing Saturday when she heard Sammy, her eight-year-old Catahoula, barking wildly outside the back door. Startled by Sammy's uncharacteristic behavior, Kay rushed out to see the cause of all the commotion and found herself face to face with a rattlesnake that had taken up residence in her flowerbed.

From that point on, it was fast-forward and slow motion both at the same time. Kay, initially paralyzed by fear, finally screamed. The snake, startled by the noise, sprang forward. Anticipating the reptile's reaction, Sammy leapt between the snake and her master, protecting Kay from the full brunt of the snake's wrath. In so doing, Sammy became the pincushion for the rattler's fangs.

Harrison gushed her appreciation for her faithful canine's bravery to *The Arizona Republic*. "She saved my life.... She got between me and the snake."

However, immediately following the incident, there wasn't time to demonstrate any kind of thanks. Instead, Kay needed to get her faithful pooch to a vet, and judging by Sammy's condition, that visit couldn't come soon enough. Sammy's head began to swell, and before too long the pup became lethargic. Kay saw that her protector was in pain; it was all Kay could do to haul Sammy into her car. By the time she arrived at the vet clinic, one of Sammy's eyes was completely swollen shut.

It was five long days before Sammy was finally released from the doggy hospital and back at home with a very grateful Kay. As it turned out, Sammy wasn't the only hero in the story. Had Kay not had the foresight to ensure her beloved pet received a snakebite vaccine the previous summer, one veterinarian suggested Sammy might have not survived the ordeal.

It's important for dog owners to understand the necessity of snake-proofing their pets and discouraging aggressive behavior between Fido and any slithering creature happening along. At the same time, when it comes down to protecting oneself and one's family, some of us will stop at nothing.

And in the animal kingdom, nothing is more important than family. Thank heaven our canine friends number their human masters in that sacred unit.

Finding a Measure of Peace Amid Turmoil

A dog will teach you unconditional love. If you can have that in your life, things won't be too bad.

—Robert Wagner, actor

THEY'RE CALLED COURTHOUSE DOGS, and the idea for using these animals to help victims of crime make their way through difficult courtroom situations has been around in the U.S. for several years now. It was an idea that evolved out of a series of innocent, unplanned events involving Washington State Attorney Ellen O'Neill-Stephens and her own golden retriever, Jeeter, in 2003.

Jeeter was a trained service dog that had been adopted into O'Neill-Stephens' family to assist the attorney's son, Sean, who suffered from cerebral palsy, with the activities of daily living. Because Sean's schedule was such that there were days when Jeeter was at home by himself, O'Neill-Stephens began taking the dog to work with her so he wasn't spending those days alone.

The legal cases O'Neill-Stephens typically dealt with involved emotionally charged circumstances, such as sexual assault and abuse. Over time, it became clear that Jeeter's presence was a calming factor when O'Neill-Stephens discussed cases with her clients, asking them to share what they'd experienced, and even during times of defense cross-examination. It took a while, but eventually everyone involved started to notice how the temperament in a room was so different when Jeeter was present, and it wasn't long before one or another attorney actually requested the dog during certain challenging situations.

One particularly difficult case involved two seven-year-old girls who were testifying against their father in a sexual abuse case. One news story reported that the girls were so overwhelmed by their situation that they were in danger of crumbling emotionally. When asked to share their story, they cried and refused to take the stand. That's when Jeeter was brought in see if he could calm the girls. And it worked. The girls were able to testify, and the case had a favorable outcome. This story resulted in the juvenile department bringing in a service dog on a permanent, full-time basis.

But the experience with Jeeter didn't only get the ball rolling in Seattle, Washington, and throughout that state. O'Neill-Stephens' dog was the catalyst that encouraged other courthouses across the United States to pause and take notice. In retrospect, it was Psychology 101—people who've been abused, abandoned and left to fend for themselves need some feeling of security if they are to conquer their past and find the strength to move forward. Courthouse dogs like Jeeter, who could provide the kind of unconditional support that victims might not perceive is available to them, are invaluable in building a bridge where none previously existed.

In 2008, Courthouse Dogs, LLC, was officially founded in Washington, with the organization's mandate set on "promoting justice through the use of well-trained dogs to provide emotional support to all in the criminal justice system." Today, courthouse dogs are common in Texas, California, Florida, Missouri and Michigan, but the program is still in its infancy. Although Jeeter and other dogs like her were a natural at the job, O'Neill-Stephens recognized that in order to make the concept succeed in courtrooms and ensure every experience between victims and courthouse dogs is a positive one, a set of best practices needed to be developed. To that end, Courthouse Dogs, LLC, decided that dogs had to have the following criteria to eventually make it to the end of their training: they needed to be "quiet, unobtrusive, and emotionally available," able to sit for prolonged periods of time and not prone to distracting the witness or others during the proceedings.

There was also a lot to consider when pairing up a potential witness with a courthouse dog. Sitting in a courtroom and coming up against someone you think might have wronged you is stressful in any circumstance. That didn't mean a courthouse dog was beneficial in every situation. According to the standards of Courthouse Dogs, LLC, using this support "should be reserved for only those witnesses that truly require this assistance."

O'Neill-Stephens and her colleagues at Courthouse Dogs, LLC, also agreed that canine candidates for this position must be specially trained and that it should not be assumed that a therapy dog was necessarily qualified to be a courthouse dog. One of the reasons for this distinction is that a therapy dog is usually emotionally, and often physically, tied to one individual; courthouse dogs, on the other hand, need to be flexible. They must be empathetic and able to connect with new people quickly. At the same time, they must be disciplined enough to know what's expected of them, even when their "master" isn't close by. These dogs also must be reliable enough to follow through with what they have been trained to do in every circumstance.

Today, five years after O'Neill-Stephens first introduced the concept of allowing a dog into the courtroom, there is a long list of requirements for any animal that is considered for the training. It's important these requirements are met; O'Neill-Stephens repeatedly emphasizes that a single bad experience could mean a huge setback for the program, or threaten to squelch it altogether. Not every cute and cuddly pooch makes it in the courtroom.

That's why the dogs in the stories that follow are so special.

A Boy's Best Friend

*The reason why a dog has so many friends is
because he wags his tail instead of his tongue.*

–Anonymous

IT'S A BASIC TENET OF LAW throughout North America
that defendants have the right to face their accusers,
regardless the charge or circumstance. Given
that cases of wrongful conviction—whether they
be because an accuser made an honest mistake or
because of outright perjury—are not uncommon,
the idea of facing your accuser, at least in theory,
sounds like a good one.

Should any of us find ourselves victimized physically, mentally or emotionally by an individual,
we would be hard-pressed to imagine the anxiety
we'd feel sitting across from the accused in a packed
courtroom, having to tell our story, and later, being
cross-examined by a defense attorney looking for
holes in our testimony. For some victims, the
trauma caused by this interaction is enough to dis-
suade them from testifying, even if that means the
accused goes free.

That was almost the situation in a case involving
a five-year-old boy in the United States, known to the
media as Joey. Joey and his mother, Sophia, were
victims of domestic violence. The youngster had
watched his dad, Robert, beat on his mother more
times than he could remember, but it was the most
recent attack that he was asked to tell the court about.

Sitting in a courtroom and explaining to a bunch of strangers how his dad brutalized his mother over and over again and how he, no matter how hard he tried, couldn't stop him, so frightened Joey that he flatly refused to take the stand. Since the police had been called to the scene, Sophia had been subpoenaed to testify against her husband, and she agreed that she would uphold that court order, even though she was also reluctant to speak out. And prosecuting attorney Tomas Gahan had enough experience at domestic assault trials to know it was quite common for a woman to downplay her abuse.

On the other hand, Joey had not had the time nor the practice to distance himself from the emotional effect of the situation and therefore could have a huge impact on the case. Gahan knew that he had to find a way to gently encourage Joey to share his story, and Gahan had an idea that might work.

One Gentle Giant

In talking with the boy, Gahan learned Joey loved dogs, puppies especially. It just so happened that the prosecutor's office could avail themselves of trained assistance dogs. Gahan had one dog in particular in mind. The golden retriever named Ellie was far from a puppy, but her accommodating and gentle disposition provided an extraordinary measure of comfort to those with whom she came into contact. She had spent the first three years of her life being trained for these types of situations: to calm witnesses and victims of violent crime during their presence in the courtroom and while they testified. Gahan thought perhaps Ellie could give Joey the comfort and confidence the boy needed to answer questions.

With the promise of meeting Ellie, Gahan moved forward to the first step in the proceedings. Sophia and Joey met with Gahan, and Gahan asked each of them to tell him what happened on the day the police showed up at their home. If Joey could make it through the defense interview, Gahan knew the youngster would be one step closer to being able to testify at trial. At first, Joey was visibly upset. But when Gahan brought Ellie into the office, and after a few moments of getting to know one another, it was clear that Joey had relaxed somewhat. He managed to tell those gathered everything that had happened and how the police found him hiding from the storm that was his life in a dark bedroom.

Gahan was relieved they'd overcome that first hurdle, but he knew there were several more to come and that at any step during the process Joey could freeze up, resulting in the worst-case scenario—Robert could be released, and he could continue to terrorize the boy and his mother.

The next step in the process was for Joey to undergo a competency hearing that would determine if the five-year-old could understand the difference between telling the truth and a lie. Thanks to Ellie, who kept Joey relaxed throughout his interview with the judge, Joey passed, and the judge allowed the boy to testify at his father's upcoming trial.

It's most often months before an accused makes it to the courtroom. Time can dim memories and weaken resolves. Sophia was still responsible for testifying, but if Joey changed his mind at any moment, there was really nothing anyone could do about it. Gahan was grateful to see that when the trial came, Joey seemed confident, especially since he was allowed to have Ellie by his side.

Finally, it was Joey's turn to take the stand. Ellie was nearby, giving the boy all the moral support he needed, and Joey looked strong, fearless even. And then the unthinkable happened. Joey's aunt on his father's side entered the courtroom. The two made eye contact and, suddenly, Joey lost all his nerve. He froze and wouldn't tell Gahan what had upset him.

It was Ellie's presence that eventually calmed Joey down enough for him to share his concerns with Gahan and the judge in judge's chambers; the judge asked Joey's aunt to leave the courtroom, relieving Joey's anxiety. From that point on, there was no stopping the young lad. With Ellie by his side, giving the boy an encouraging lick every so often and rolling over for a tummy rub, Joey was able to give his testimony to the court and clearly and assertively deal with any questions from defense counsel. Joey's testimony was a huge factor in his father receiving a seven-year sentence for his abusive behavior.

It appeared that Joey's concerns about his aunt were founded—she and the rest of her family were angry with Joey and his mother. In a conversation following Robert's sentencing, Sophia told Gahan that "she and Joey were living together in an apartment and that they were alone now because everyone in their family hated them." At the same time, she was quick to point out that "for the first time in their lives they felt free."

Were it not for Ellie's presence throughout the proceedings, the result could have been a very different one.

First and Foremost

In October 2007, a golden retriever named Sam was chosen as one of six PetSmart Heroes in Maricopa County. Sam earned the title because of his role as the first courthouse dog in the county, and the support he'd provided through the years wasn't something that anyone could have imagined prior to Sam coming on the scene. But he wasn't the only dog serving in this capacity.

Moose, an ancient breed of dog called a Thai Ridgeback, also has a proven track record as a good listener and soft shoulder. In March 2010, the *Arizona Republic* reported how Moose stood beside a nine-year-old in Maricopa County who was taking the stand to testify against his accused molester. Thanks to Moose's comforting presence, which could mean something as simple as his warm body hovering close by, the boy was able to share his nightmare and contend with cross-examination.

Reporter Melanie Kiser told how, following the trial, the boy stretched out on the floor and started to cry, the stress of the day just spilling out of him. Without any hesitation or direction, Moose ambled over to the child, sat beside him and "put his paws around him and licked the tears off his face." The scene vividly spelled out what the courthouse dog program was all about. There were no words that could translate that picture of Moose and the boy—it was a "you had to be there to understand it" moment.

In the end, the stress was all worth it; the boy's molester received a 54-year prison sentence, the boy survived his ordeal and Moose went on to help the next victim of crime.

Courthouse Dogs Today

Since the initial instance of using courthouse dogs in 2003, dogs have appeared in courtrooms throughout the United States, and the program is growing. Dogs have been used in other capacities besides courtrooms, such as at the Baltimore Child Abuse Center; they've demonstrated a proven track record when it comes to dealing with victims of extreme wrongdoing.

Puppy candidates for the program are initially placed into appropriate living arrangements, where caregivers are expected to follow a rigid training schedule. Once they are old enough, usually around the one-year mark, they are moved to a training center such as Canine Companions for Independence.

In time, and where possible, these dogs are placed in courthouses throughout the United States.

Other renditions of the courthouse dog program are also being established. In February 2010, Kathleen Gray wrote about the "Paws and Order: SDU" program in *USA Today*. Dogs in this program don't always accompany witnesses to trial, nor do they always sit in during all interview sessions. But they do meet with children who've experienced violence. "…it's just amazing to see the smile on their faces and how much less stress they have after playing with the dogs," said Harris County Assistant District Attorney Donna Hawkins.

The idea of bringing an animal into a courthouse might seem foreign to some, and downright ridiculous to others, but for people such as Joey and Sophia, and the countless other victims of abuse and assault who've found comfort in these dogs' presence and the courage to speak out, dogs like Sam, Moose and Ellie are heroes of the highest order.

(NOTE: The exact locations of these courtroom stories have been purposely withheld, and the names of the victims have been changed in order to protect and respect their privacy.)

Dialing 9-1-1: A Lifesaving Skill

We do not so much need the help of our friends as the confidence of their help in need.

–Epicurus, philosopher, 3rd century BC

SEASONED 9-1-1 OPERATORS, especially those who cover areas with large populations, are used to receiving all kinds of emergency calls. In many communities throughout North America, 9-1-1 calls are dispatched through regional headquarters such the Phoenix Fire Department Regional Dispatch Center (PFDRDC). The PFDRDC provides service for 20 jurisdictions covering 2000 square miles within Maricopa County, including the city of Scottsdale, Arizona.

With a population estimated at about 245,500, the city's 9-1-1 operators could be kept quite busy responding to emergency calls. But it wasn't the busyness that had colleagues talking on September 11, 2008. What really had the work-room buzzing was that the 9-1-1 operators in the "West's most western town" received perhaps one of the most unusual of the roughly 300,000 calls they receive in any given year.

It was a call that thankfully resulted in a happy ending.

Summer 2007

When Joe Stalnaker chose an eight-week-old German shepherd puppy as his newest pet, it was with two considerations in mind: the former soldier was looking for a faithful companion as well as one that he could train to perform special duties. It was going to be Buddy's job to look out for Stalnaker and provide him with a measure of autonomy, something that a person with Stalnaker's unique medical needs would find invaluable.

Stalnaker's story really began 10 years earlier when, while serving in the military, he suffered a severe head injury that caused him to experience unpredictable seizures. While some seizures can manifest themselves in a fairly mild way, others can be crippling. A serious seizure can cause sudden involuntary muscle contractions, propelling its victim into a dangerous situation or an immediate loss of consciousness. Seizures lasting more than five minutes are classified as a medical emergency.

Stalnaker regularly experienced seizures, and they could be debilitating. When this occurred, it was paramount that he receive medical attention as soon as possible, something that doesn't always happen when an individual is home alone and goes through this type of medical trauma. Stalnaker was hoping Buddy would eventually learn to recognize the onset of a seizure, perhaps even warning Stalnaker of the impending crisis, and follow through with specific tasks aimed at getting Stalnaker the help he needed. The spin-off benefit meant that Stalnaker could maintain his independence. In effect, the one-time military man wanted Buddy to become more than just a companion: he was hoping Buddy would develop into a specialized assistance dog.

Service dogs have been used for decades to assist people with special challenges, but the movement to teach these animals the particular skills necessary to help individuals suffering from seizures only began to take root in the 1980s. According to the Epilepsy Foundation, knowing that dogs could be used in this way was somewhat of an accidental discovery. One woman realized that some dogs might have the unique talent of recognizing when their owners were about to experience a seizure after she noticed her own dog seemed to be able to forecast when she was about to have one.

Anxious to test the theory, service dog workers began to train and test suitable dogs, and it wasn't long before the term "seizure dog" was coined to describe the unique work these specially trained dogs did. British neuropsychiatrist and epilepsy specialist Dr. Stephen W. Brown worked alongside animal trainer Val Strong in developing techniques to help these dogs sense when their masters were about to experience a seizure. The duo trained dogs to remain with their masters throughout the ordeal, and most importantly, taught the dogs to dial 9-1-1 and bark loudly into the telephone receiver to alert the dispatcher that there was a problem at the location associated with that number. In 1999, a story highlighting Brown and Strong's work appeared in *Seizure–European Journal of Epilepsy*. And while there is always a measure of risk that a dog won't perform the way a client or the dog's trainers would expect, the experiment into this unique use of a dog's talents proved to be priceless for many epileptics and others who suffered from seizures.

Stalnaker was hoping his experience with Buddy would be one of the priceless varieties; he wasn't disappointed.

September 2008

By the fall of 2008, Stalnaker and Buddy had developed a close relationship. After 16 months of living together, the German shepherd had proven he was both smart and faithful. Stalnaker himself had trained the dog to respond to his unique needs, and Buddy had performed fabulously.

That morning in September might have started off much like any other, but it was soon apparent that Buddy was going to have to use everything he'd learned if Stalnaker was to live to enjoy the full colors of the season.

Before the incident even happened, Buddy knew something wasn't right. The normally quiet, attentive dog was anxiously watching his master as Stalnaker made his way through his morning routine. Sometime before noon, Stalnaker suffered a full-blown seizure.

That was when Buddy's training kicked in, and he sprang into action.

Knocking over the telephone, Buddy did what Stalnaker had painstakingly trained the dog to do: he called 9-1-1. Using his teeth, Buddy repeatedly pressed the keypad button that was programmed to dial 9-1-1 until he finally made a connection with emergency personnel. When the operator answered and asked for a description of the emergency, Buddy barked. He barked again, and then again, even after Chris Trott, the dispatcher who took the call, asked if there was anyone near the phone who could come on the line.

Because Stalnaker's address was flagged in the emergency system as a residence with an assistance dog capable of calling 9-1-1, police were immediately dispatched to the man's home. In fact, Buddy had called 9-1-1 twice before that, and as recently as a month earlier. Still, Buddy's unique talent was the talk of the day and was something most emergency responders hadn't witnessed firsthand before. "It's pretty incredible," Scottsdale police sergeant Mark Clark told reporters. "Even the veteran dispatchers—they haven't heard of anything like this."

Stalnaker spent the next two days recovering in the hospital. But thanks to Buddy, the man was able to return home again.

"Buddy, he basically gives me my independence," Stalnaker told reporters from *The Arizona Republic* after he'd recovered from his ordeal. "He's my world. He's my best friend, no question. He's always there, and I just hope I can be as good to him as he's been to me."

Other 9-1-1 Heroes

Buddy certainly isn't the only dog who has learned to recognize its owner's special health needs and respond appropriately. Brown and Strong's work has provided individuals in similar circumstances with yet another tool that makes it possible for them to maintain their freedom and dignity.

On March 13, 1996, CNN reported a story coming out of Nashua, New Hampshire, about a woman named Judy Bayly who found herself in what could have been a life-threatening situation. Bayly relied on a special machine to help monitor her breathing throughout the night, and in the wee hours of March 12, the apparatus started beeping wildly.

The alarm roused Bayly's eight-year-old Irish setter, Lyric. The well-trained dog knew what that sound meant—it meant the machine had malfunctioned somehow, and Bayly might not be receiving the oxygen she needed.

Lyric didn't need any prompting to know what to do next; she'd done it at least once before. Rushing to the telephone, the setter activated the pre-programmed button that would dial 9-1-1 for her. When Nashua Fire Rescue dispatcher Charlene Hall answered the phone, she was greeted with the sounds of a barking dog.

By the time medical personnel arrived, Bayly was in the throes of a full-blown asthma attack. Thanks to her faithful canine, Bayly survived.

~∞~

In 2004, news agencies as far away as Minneapolis-St. Paul ran stories about 45-year-old Leana Beasley of Richland, Washington, and the amazing Rottweiler named Faith who saved the woman's life.

Throughout much of the day on September 7, Faith was inordinately clingy and whiny, giving Leana an uneasy feeling that perhaps her dog had noticed something that Leana wasn't aware of. Faith had a unique ability to smell when there was a change in Leana's body chemistry, something that frequently preceded the grand mal seizures she was prone to experiencing. Leana, recognizing that Faith had sensed an impending seizure, decided to return to the safety of her wheelchair. Leana fell to the floor before she could remind Faith to call 9-1-1.

But Faith didn't need the reminder.

Like a well-oiled machine clicking into action, Faith knocked the phone over and pushed the 9-1-1-designated speed dial with her nose. Again, when the call was answered, Faith started barking and continued to bark until she was certain the person on the other end understood what was going on. Faith then returned to her owner's side and rolled the woman into a recovery position to ensure Leana could breathe well and wouldn't choke on her own saliva or other bodily fluids.

Of course, when emergency personnel arrived at the home, Leana was in no position to let them in. However, Faith managed to unlock the door, allowing paramedics to enter and provide her mistress with the life-saving care she so desperately needed.

Faith's rise above and beyond the call of duty was so astonishing that she was not only recognized by the local Benton County Emergency Services people with a Certificate of Recognition but was also the first "non-human recipient" of the American Red Cross' Real Hero Award. In addition, Faith went on to win a 2005 American Kennel Club Award for Canine Excellence.

While someone with a medical challenge can purchase dogs who are trained for the kinds of service these animals performed, it's interesting to note that each of these dogs were pets first—beloved companions lovingly trained by the owners they served. The time and attention pet owners spend on teaching their pets the necessary skills to meet their special needs is extraordinary.

But then again, so are these pets.

Feisty Felines

As anyone who has ever been around a cat for any length of time well knows, cats have enormous patience with the limitations of the human mind.

–Cleveland Amory, American author and
animal rights activist

Comfort and Commitment

If you are worthy of its affection, a cat will be your friend, but never your slave.

–Theophile Gautier, French writer

THE PRACTICE OF KEEPING DOMESTICATED cats began almost 10,000 years ago. The felines were beautiful to look at, affectionate to their owners and, more importantly, undemanding, making them wonderful companions. These independent creatures came and went as they pleased, kept themselves clean and didn't need much looking after.

Ancient civilizations also believed a cat was a talisman of sorts, bringing good luck to its owner and possessing magical abilities. Perhaps this was one of the motivating factors that led the Egyptians to bring cats aboard their Nile boats. It was a practice that continued and expanded over the centuries, until just about any seafaring vessel worth its salt had a cat on board.

A good ship's cat was believed to lick its fur against the grain to warn its shipmates of an impending hailstorm; predict rain with a sneeze; get all frisky when expecting a wild wind; start a hailstorm with the magic in its tail; prevent a sea-faring disaster; protect its crew; and even predict good or bad luck for approaching sailors. Of course, cats were valuable for more practical reasons as well. Cats chase mice and rats. A good mouser on a long sea voyage is critical for the crew's health and well-being.

Cartographer Matthew Flinders knew the value of having a cat onboard when he mapped Australia's coastline between 1801 and 1803. His cat, Trim, was a great mouser, a faithful companion and, for his longstanding service, was named the first cat to travel around Australia on a ship. The crew of the RMS *Empress of Ireland,* on the other hand, should have taken better heed of their cat. On May 28, 1914, after sailing on every voyage the *Empress* had made to that point in its history, the ship's cat Emmy reportedly refused to board. The ship left anyway and sank the next day.

During wartime, several different species of animals, and even birds, played a particularly important role in the lives of a ship's crew. Of course, army and navy regulations didn't always allow for animals onboard wartime vessels. That didn't stop 17-year-old George Hickinbottom.

Everybody's Pet

The Ordinary Seaman was about to hit the high seas in March 1948, a few years after a truce was called in a war that involved every world power and that proved to be perhaps more brutal than the global conflict two decades earlier. World War II was a turbulent time—a time that tested the valor of every able-bodied young person who joined the fight for peace. A few years after the war, the memories of courage and the stories of valiant heroism still fueled a nation.

At the same time, George Hickinbottom was really just a youth. Although he predicted a safer voyage for himself than those of his comrades of only a few years earlier, he knew he would miss the comforts of home and family, and undoubtedly the prospect of the voyage itself was frightening. And so when Hickinbottom happened upon a mangy kitten barely a year old stumbling about along the naval dockyards of Stonecutters Island, it's understandable that his heart was touched. Fancying a special companion, someone to love along the journey, the young seaman stuffed the frightened feline into his coat and smuggled him onboard the British frigate, the HMS *Amethyst*.

Young Simon might have started out as Hickinbottom's pet cat, but it was clear his loyalties weren't limited to his new owner. As he gained

weight and his fur took on a healthy glow, his disposition blossomed as well. Soon, Simon was
everybody's best friend. Even the officers couldn't
argue against the value of having such a creature
onboard. Aside from centuries of superstition
arguing the benefits of a ship having a resident cat,
Simon brought the lonely sailors comfort.

Simon also managed to endear himself to the
ship's captain, Lieutenant Commander Ian
Griffiths. Because Hickinbottom had been named
Chief Captain of the Forecastle, making sure
everything was in working order was his responsibility. The position placed him in constant proximity
to the captain, and their quarters were close to one
another. Although Hickinbottom was able to keep
Simon's presence onboard a secret for a time,
it wasn't long before Griffiths and Simon bumped
into one another. It was a good thing that Griffiths
had a soft spot for cats because Simon didn't get
the boot. Instead, an olive branch had been
extended, and Simon was allowed to secure his
position as mouser with the crew of the *Amethyst*.

He was a darned good mouser, too. Nary a rodent
entered the cook's pantry, so no stores were lost to
pests, and the potential for spreading disease was
reduced. Simon was also pretty good at making sure
his efforts were recognized, depositing much of his
carnage at the good Captain Griffiths' feet—or on
his bunk!

Yes, Simon took to his new job like the *Amethyst* took to the sea. And true to a cat's unobtrusive temperament, Simon was no trouble whatsoever. Hickinbottom and his shipmates complied with the captain's charge that any "muck" left behind by the feline was to be cleared up immediately, and Simon's gentle disposition was calming to anyone who came into contact with him. It wasn't long before Simon was named the *Amethyst*'s official mascot—much later his shipmates honored him with the title of "Able Seacat."

The Changing Tide

For the first part of Simon's tenure on the *Amethyst,* it was fairly smooth sailing. But the tide started to turn later in 1948 with the departure of Captain Griffiths and the introduction of Captain Bernard Skinner. Luckily, Simon endeared himself to Griffiths' replacement in short order and continued his employ as if nothing had changed.

April 1949 brought a considerably more difficult challenge for cat and crew. The *Amethyst* had been posted to Nanking, the capital city of the Republic of China at the time. The ship's mission was to report to duty along the volatile Yangtze River and relieve another ship previously charged with guarding the British Embassy from the rising tensions between Chinese Communists and the Chinese Nationalist Party and the ensuing civil war being played out there.

On April 20, the *Amethyst* was the target of heavy fire from hostile soldiers along the north bank. The ship was damaged and ran aground on nearby Rose Island. After receiving more than 50 hits, the ship wasn't the only thing with holes in it. Twelve men were reportedly wounded, and another 15 seamen lost their lives in the battle. Captain Skinner was wounded and later died from his injuries.

There was one more casualty that day. Simon was seriously injured.

When the badly burned mouser was discovered, having dragged himself topside despite the many shrapnel wounds dotting his small body, medical staff did everything they could to ease his suffering. They cleaned and bandaged his burns and removed shrapnel, but they really didn't expect the cat to survive. In fact, the day he was discovered, medical staff predicted he wouldn't make it through that first night.

Of course, with the expected nine lives and all, Simon had considerably different ideas on the matter. Instead of rolling over and giving up, Simon was working harder than ever. Now that the ship had run aground, rats were invading it. While the sailors maintained their positions, Simon captured and killed at the very least a rat a day, keeping a check on the ever-growing rat population.

Simon discovered another calling. Not only did the crew enjoy watching him hunt, but the cat's presence also built morale among the battered crew. The *Amethyst's* medical officer believed the men relegated to sickbay would benefit by Simon's company, and so the cat spent a few hours each day snuggling up to one or another of the wounded, easing their tension in the process. At other times during the *Amethyst*'s posting, Simon paired up with the crew's dog, a terrier named Peggy, to cheer up the men.

It took Simon a little longer, however, to win the loyalties of Captain Skinner's replacement. Lieutenant Commander John Kerans wasn't all that keen on cats and didn't really want one on a ship in his charge. Up until Kerans' arrival, Simon had made his home in the captain's quarters, having moved over from Hickinbottom's bunk early on in his employ as king cat. The *Amethyst*'s new captain, however, would have none of that. Kerans booted Simon off his bed every time the cat managed to sneak in—a situation that disturbed the young tom to no end. Simon couldn't figure Kerans out. Why was the man so adverse to the cat's presence? Hadn't Simon presented the new captain with enough dead rats to prove his loyalties?

Finally, after Kerans found himself laid up for a few days with a case of the flu, Simon managed to crack through the man's protective armor. With little to no energy available for Kerans to boot Simon off his bed, the cat curled up. Kerans must have found comfort in the gentle creature, just like his men had in sickbay. It's not clear what might have caused the change in Kerans' attitude toward the mouser, but from that time on, Simon never had to worry about being evicted from the captain's quarters.

The First of Many Honors

Simon kept himself busy after his wounds healed, but it was clear that he wasn't as strong as he used to be. With that in mind, the ship's crew decided to lend the cat a helping hand when it came to one particularly large and destructive rat nicknamed "Mao Tse Tung." The crew had set numerous traps for the rodent, thinking it was too large and powerful for the still-ailing Simon, but again, Simon had other plans. One day the rat had the audacity to faceoff with Simon, and the killer cat prevailed. The rat was dead, and Simon was "Able Seacat" thereafter.

Simon also became the recipient of several other medals and titles. While the *Amethyst* was making its way to port in Plymouth, on November 1, 1949, the survivors of what was becoming known as the "Yangtze Incident" were being hailed as heroes. Simon, as one of the crew, was recognized as well. The cat was nominated for the Dickin Medal. Nick Cooper, author of "Simon of the Amethyst," recounts how aggressively Captain Kerans supported the nomination:

There were a large number of rats...after two months the rats were much diminished. Throughout the Incident Simon's behavior was of the highest order. One would not have expected him to have survived a shell making a hole over a foot in diameter in a steel plate, yet after a few days Simon was as friendly as ever. Simon's presence on the ship, together with Peggy the dog, was a decided factor in maintaining the high level of morale of the ship's company. They gave the ship an air of domesticity and normality...

Simon was the first cat, and the first animal belonging to a crew of the Royal Navy, to be awarded the Dickin Medal. Established by Maria Dickin, the medal is awarded to animals that have exhibited "conspicuous gallantry and devotion to duty associated with, or under the control of, any branch of the Armed Forces or Civil Defence units."

Simon received the honor, which was rapidly referred to as the "Victoria Cross for animals," on August 10, 1949, but the actual medal—with its engraving "For Gallantry...we also serve"—would be presented to him when he returned to the UK. Both Simon and his canine shipmate, Peggy, received *Amethyst* campaign ribbons for their service.

News of Simon followed him to every port of call on his way back to Plymouth, and at each stop photographers and reporters scrambled to get a snapshot of Simon and a story for their local papers—Simon was apparently as uplifting to the reading public as the cat's presence had been to the injured men in sickbay. But on his arrival in the UK, Simon had to undergo the same indignity of every animal returning to the country—a six-month quarantine.

It was hard to imagine the independent-minded Simon living in such conditions, but there was nothing anyone could do about it. In due time, Simon was scheduled to receive his award and a life of retirement with Captain Kerans.

The Final Boarding Call

Unfortunately, such a cheery end to a life of service was not in the cards for the tom. In November 1949, just a few weeks into his quarantine, the cat spiked a fever and was diagnosed with a virus. The veterinarian charged with his care surmised that the cat had succumbed to his illness because his heart had been weakened during the attack on the *Amethyst*. Either way, the cat that had brought so much joy to a crew full of men under such trying conditions had kneaded his last pillow. He was buried at the People's Dispensary for Sick Animals cemetery at Ilford, Essex. Simon's gravestone reads:

In Memory of "SIMON"
Served in H.M.S. Amethyst
May 1948 – November 1949
Awarded Dickin Medal August 1949
Died 28th November 1949
"Throughout the Yangtze incident his behaviour
was of the highest order."

In the end, Simon did receive the Dickin Award posthumously, with the following citation:

Able Seaman Simon, for distinguished and meritorious service on HMS Amethyst, *you are hereby awarded the Distinguished* Amethyst *Campaign Ribbon.*

Be it known that on April 26, 1949, though recovering from wounds, when HMS Amethyst *was standing by off Rose Bay you did single-handedly and unarmed stalk down and destroy "Mao Tse Tung," a rat guilty of raiding food supplies which were critically short.*

*Be it further known that from April 22 to August 4
you did rid HMS Amethyst of pestilence and vermin,
with unrelenting faithfulness.*

In the weeks following Simon's death, condolences
and fan mail continued to pour in to the navy, the
People's Dispensary for Sick Animals and to Captain
Kerans personally. To this day, the cat with the gentle disposition and fierce independence who touched
so many lives and served so valiantly against all
odds still captures the imagination of animal lovers
who hear his story. In November 2007, the Royal
Navy held a special ceremony in the cat's honor,
remembering his courage during his suffering.
As Robert W. Green said during a tribute to the cat
in May 2008, Simon is "so long gone from our lives,
but never absent from our hearts."

Everyone Needs a Little Faith

*All things bright and beautiful,
All creatures great and small,
All things wise and wonderful,
The Lord God made them all…*

–Cecil Frances Alexander, hymn-writer and poet

THERE WAS A TIME WHEN SOME religious folks didn't readily
like cats, and many historians suggest part of the
reason for this mistrust was that the ancient
Egyptians were the first to domesticate these lovely

creatures—they even elevated them to the status of "sacred" animal in that culture's history. Since early Biblical times, the Egyptians ruled over the Israelites, so it's understandable that the Hebrew people viewed with skepticism anything closely associated with the Egyptians.

Over the centuries, cats as sacred vertebrates have assumed positions of power in various mythologies and belief systems. In some cases, these religious associations served to create an ever-increasing mistrust of these poor creatures. For example, the cat's association to the historically misunderstood practice of Wicca cemented, in many people's minds, a negative view of the animal. Perhaps this is why some members of the Christian church at one time thought of cats as "agents of the devil," and the felines weren't welcome in many Christian households.

Thankfully, that has all changed. Although animal lovers attempt to tame any number of species into becoming household companions, today, cats are neck-and-neck in popularity with dogs as the pet of choice in most First World countries.

For the people of St. Augustine and St. Faith's Church in London, England, back in the days leading up to World War II, there was no question that one particularly scrawny, gray-and-white tabby was pretty special indeed.

Persistence Pays Off

There's a reason why October 29, 1929, was named Black Tuesday. For weeks before that fateful day, stocks traded on Wall Street were losing their value. Investors, noticing a trend that looked like it was going to continue, started pulling out their investments in increasingly larger numbers until that dark day when the market lost an estimated $14 billion in a single 24-hour period. The collapse of the world market left an indelible impression, and the next decade saw the world's economy plummet to such an extent that analysts have since deemed the crash of the stock market the "biggest financial crisis of the 20th century."

For more than 10 years after that Black Tuesday, times were extraordinarily tough. Families scraped together everything they could to provide their children with the barest of food rations. In Britain, unemployment figures climbed to an unprecedented 2.5 million or what amounted to 20 percent of their workforce at the time. The world was a hungry place indeed. It's no surprise, then, that when a malnourished cat, probably abandoned by an owner who could no longer afford to keep it, wandered into a London church in 1936, the verger tossed her back onto the street without a second thought. Surely the thought of taking in a stray animal and the responsibility that came along with it would appear frivolous to a congregation penny pinching to help pay the bills.

Undeterred, the cat found another way into the building—the church was a lot warmer than the back alleyways of downtown London, and with any luck at all, the people of the parish would remember the scripture that promises the dogs the crumbs from under the dinner table. The church's verger, however, was as persistent as the cat. When Thomas Evans spotted the cat a second time in the hallowed sanctuary of St. Augustine and St. Faith's Church on Watling Street, he caught her and put her back outside once again.

As they say, "third time's a charm." With dogged determination, and a clear survival of the fittest drive, the cat snuck in yet again, only to meet up directly with the now frustrated verger and the church's priest, Father Henry Ross. Before the cat had a chance to dash away, Evans swept it up into his arms and was about to set it outside when Father Ross questioned the man about his actions. Did Evans not like cats? The emaciated cat looked abandoned and hungry. Surely the church could afford to spare a little milk? After all, didn't scripture say the Lord preserves both man and beast?

Perhaps Evans was surprised at the priest's reaction, but it was a pleasant surprise. Evans' wife, Rosalind, loved cats, and he was certain she'd like to help care for the creature. And so it was decided that the cat's new home would be the church rectory, alongside Father Ross, until such time as its owner was located.

Making It Permanent

As the days slipped by and weeks became months, it became clear that whoever once owned the stray cat was not about to come forward. Father Ross had done his due diligence, letting the congregation know about the cat, advertising its presence with posters providing information on the animal and encouraging its owner to come forward to claim the feline. But Father Ross was becoming attached to the furry critter, so he wasn't too disturbed at the thought of keeping the animal. In fact, truth be told, she had more than made up for the meager rations Father Ross and the women of the church fed her by clearing the church of any unwanted mice. She was pretty affectionate too, having warmed right up to the pastor, and the parishioners also enjoyed having her around.

Of course, a good church cat looking to become part of the congregation's permanent family needed a more suitable calling card than a simple "hey you." It struck Father Ross as significant that the cat's persistence at making the church her new home demonstrated a kind of faith, and so it was decided that their newest member would be christened "Faith."

By now, Faith had made her presence known to the entire parish family, strolling along the aisles or perching herself on the front pew during church services or sitting at Father Ross' feet while he was preaching. The women of the altar-guild, along with Evans and his wife, assisted Father Ross in any way they could to help care for the parish cat, but really,

Faith was no problem whatsoever; her very presence brought added warmth to the church, and the cat was truly a blessing to have around.

The next four years passed by without incident, but in August 1940, folks were starting to notice a distinct waddle in Faith's carriage. A few too many mice, it was thought at first. But when Faith was mysteriously absent one morning and didn't greet Father Ross with her usual demands for food, the good padre started to worry. Once he'd readied himself for the day and enjoyed his breakfast tea, and Faith still hadn't shown up for any attention, Father Ross decided to go looking for her.

He found her in the first place he looked—in her basket. She was safe and sound and happy as usual, but it looked as though the cat had added another full-time job to her title of church mouser. As Father Ross bent over, he found another tuft of fur snuggled under the cat's belly. It appeared that sometime during the night Faith had become a mother!

That Sunday, the church celebrated the news of the arrival of Faith's black-and-white kitten with a joyful rendition of "All Things Bright and Beautiful." Since the kitten resembled Chi-Chi, the panda housed at the London Zoo at the time, the consensus in the congregation was that they name the baby tom, Panda.

Instinct kicked in, and Faith proved to be the perfect mother. Baby Panda grew like a bad weed. By the time he was a month old, he'd hit all the right milestones. His eyes were open, and he was starting to eat a little solid food. And he was learning how to use those wee legs of his, waddling here and there but never too far from Mama Faith's line of vision.

Everything was moving along quite predictably until, on September 6, 1940, Faith took it into her head to do something quite out of the ordinary. Faith approached Father Ross as he was working at his desk and started meowing for attention. When he stood up to see what she wanted, Faith darted toward a door leading to the ground floor. Father Ross, having opened the door for her, expected Faith's meowing to stop, but the mother kept calling for her master, looking over her shoulder to ensure he was following her down the stairs. Once she reached the main floor, Faith stood at the basement door and meowed some more. Again, Father Ross opened the door, and Faith dashed down the stairs. Scratching his head a little at the cat's strange behavior, Father Ross returned to his desk, leaving the doors open behind him.

At some point during the day. someone noticed Faith carrying her kitten down to the basement where she stayed for the remainder of the day. The only time Faith ventured back upstairs was to collect her dinner. When she was done eating, she dashed back to her baby, leaving a bewildered Father Ross with nothing left to do but follow her downstairs and see why she and Panda had opted to hide out in the dank and dusty dungeon rather than being in the warmer, cheery environment upstairs. What he found did nothing to answer any of his questions. For there, tucked away between assorted piles of books and paper, were Faith and baby Panda. Thinking Faith had momentarily lost her senses, Father Ross collected the kitten and returned him to his cozy basket.

Faith was not impressed.

Mother cat followed Father Ross back up the stairs, meowing incessantly, and as soon as the man turned his back, Faith snatched Panda by the scruff of the neck and returned to the basement corner. That night, Faith didn't attend the evening Vespers service, and when Father Ross returned home, he noticed the cat and her kitten were no longer in their basket. Father Ross collected the kitten and brought him back upstairs for a second time, but the next morning, he noticed Faith had again taken Panda to her basement hideaway.

Father Ross returned the kitten to his basket, but Faith again removed him and took him back downstairs. Mystified by the entire scenario, Father Ross decided to consult with the women of the parish. Perhaps other mothers would have an idea why Faith was behaving so strangely. After a bit of discussion on the matter, it was thought that perhaps Faith was trying to protect her youngster from some perceived danger. Instead of putting the kitten back upstairs, the women suggested to Father Ross that he move the cat's basket downstairs where Faith clearly felt more comfortable. Father Ross did so, and a very grateful Faith made her appreciation known and snuggled up to her baby.

The Turning of the Tide

Saturday, September 7, dawned much like any other morning. Father Ross carried out the usual preparations for the next day's church service; he had shut-ins to visit and a sermon to polish. In short, it was going to be a full day indeed—as it turned out, a lot more eventful than first expected. What happened over the next few days shouldn't have been such a surprise, really. At that point in time, the world had been involved in a second conflict of global proportions for more than a year, and during a war, especially one that was being fought so close to Britain, people had to be prepared for anything.

That Saturday, London experienced the first of many air raids that would characterize the next nine months of the war. More than 43,000 civilians lost their lives as a result of those bombings; 400 died that first day. And there wasn't much of a reprieve before a second air raid hit the city. That following Monday, September 9, having completed a day of business errands in nearby Westminster, Father Ross was making his way home on his bicycle when the air raid sirens started to wail, warning of another impending attack. Father Ross took refuge in one of the many shelters established for that very purpose. He spent a long night there before the raid was over and it was safe enough for him to return to the church. He'd already heard about some of the destruction caused by the latest bombings. There was another huge loss of civilian life.

The city had also sustained a lot of structural damage. While the buildings on one street survived relatively unscathed, other of the city's sentinels were no more than twisted heaps of steel and rubble. Eight churches were destroyed the night of September 9, and as Father Ross maneuvered his way amid the burning ruins, he could only hope his beloved church had been spared.

Such was not the case.

Father Ross arrived on Watling Street only to find his church flattened, save the church tower and a few assorted timber splinters supporting a nearly collapsed roof. A fire was still raging among the debris as Father Ross rushed out onto the site. One of the firefighters at the scene ushered him away, but after Father Ross introduced himself and assured the crew that no human victims needed to be accounted for, he continued to search for the two small creatures who were as precious to him as any other. Somewhere in the smoldering mass were Faith and her kitten, and Father Ross was determined to see if the pair had survived their ordeal.

Risking all for his beloved Faith, and ignoring the firefighters' warnings, Father Ross searched the hot coals, pushing one board aside and then another. After yelling out Faith's name a few times, Father Ross thought he heard a muffled response. Could Faith have survived the blast? Moving closer to the muted meowing, and glancing overhead at the church roof that threatened to collapse at any moment, Father Ross rushed to the corner where Faith had stowed her kitten only days earlier. Sure enough, safe in her basket was a grateful Faith with a very hungry Panda nursing at her side.

Father Ross scooped the two animals into his arms and returned to the street moments before the church roof collapsed. The padre later told reporters that when he found Faith, she was "singing such a song of praise and thanksgiving as I had never heard." Undoubtedly, Faith was grateful for Father Ross' reluctance to believe she and Panda had perished and for his persistence in finding them. But he was only one of the heroes that day. Were it not for Faith's mother instincts and the determination she displayed from her first introduction to Father Ross, as well as her repeated and defiant trips carting Panda downstairs, both mother and kitten would have died. Taking shelter downstairs, which gave the cats some protection from the bomb blasts, and remaining still despite all the noise and confusion were the two things that worked together to save Faith and Panda.

Although the majority of the church was destroyed, Father Ross' spirits soared knowing he could move forward with his companion still at his side. It took almost two months of renovations, but on November 1, Father Ross was able to hold small church services in the chapel located in the remaining church tower. Faith resumed her rightful place at her master's side, overseeing the congregation as he preached, and when Panda was old enough, he was adopted out to a nursing home.

Sharing the Story

Father Ross made a formal record of Faith's bravery in a small tribute he erected in St. Augustine and St. Faith's chapel. Ross wrote a testimonial about Faith's actions and hung it underneath a framed photograph of the cat:

"Faith" Our dear little church cat of St. Augustine and St. Faith. The bravest cat in the world. On Monday, September 9th, 1940, she endured horrors and perils beyond the power of words to tell. Shielding her kitten in a sort of recess in the house (a spot she selected three days before the tragedy occurred), she sat the whole frightful night of bombing and fire, guarding her little kitten. The roofs and masonry exploded. The whole house blazed. Four floors fell through in front of her. Fire and water and ruin all round her. Yet she stayed calm and steadfast and waited for help. We rescued her in the early morning while the place was still burning, and By the mercy of Almighty God, she and her kitten were not only saved, but unhurt. God be praised and thanked for His goodness and mercy to our dear little pet.

Everyone who came into the chapel read of Faith's story, and pretty soon the news of her bravery spread throughout the city. There was no doubt that Faith was held in high regard by Father Ross and the people of the church he served, but in 1945, Rosalind noticed a story about a dog who'd been awarded a medal for bravery. Beauty, a wire-haired terrier working with the People's Dispensary for Sick Animals (PDSA) Rescue Squad, was a pioneer in the field of animal rescue. On January 12, 1945, the dog was awarded the Dickin Medal for locating buried air-raid victims. It was an honorable and dangerous job, and Beauty performed it selflessly. Certainly, she deserved recognition for her efforts.

But Rosalind thought Faith deserved more official recognition, too. Faith's story demonstrated selfless devotion to her helpless kitten; Faith's story was an example of unconditional love and as such provided a beacon of light in a dark and hurting world. So on Faith's behalf, Rosalind wrote to Maria Elisabeth Dickin, the founder of the PDSA and the Dickin Medal, and petitioned for the cat to become a recipient of the same award.

Maria Dickin was touched by Faith's story, but there was a snag in Rosalind's idea. The animal bravery award was only given to animals recognized for "acts of animal bravery or exceptional devotion to duty" and was reserved for animals in some kind of formal service. Since its inception, the Dickin Medal had come to be known as the "animals' Victoria Cross." It wasn't until 2001 that a civilian equivalent was established with the PDSA Gold Medal, but in 1945, that option wasn't available.

Still, Maria was determined to recognize Faith's actions in some way, and she created a one-of-a-kind silver medal for the cat. And on October 12 of that year, Maria Dickin arrived at St. Augustine and St. Faith's church to present the beloved feline with her medal for "steadfast courage in the Battle of London, September 9, 1940" during a formal service that boasted such dignitaries as the Archbishop of Canterbury himself!

Faith reveled in the attention, and news agencies as far away as New York printed stories about the brave mamma.

Saying Goodbye

Although no one ever nailed down the story on Faith's early days before coming to Father Ross and the congregation he served, it was believed she was about 14 years old when she died on September 28, 1948. Faith had spent that morning with her master, taking her breakfast alongside him as she always did and curling up nearby his desk as he worked. But when Father Ross moved from the desk, he noticed Faith didn't follow. After a lifetime of dedicated service, Faith had drifted into a sleep that she wouldn't wake from in this world.

Father Ross was devastated by his loss. So were the people of his parish. The good Father held a small, memorial service for his beloved pet. It was a somber day when an entire congregation bid farewell to a small animal of great courage who not only saved the life of her beloved kitten but also touched the hearts of everyone at St. Augustine and St. Faith's. As the group gave thanks for Faith's life and service to her church family, Father Ross led the procession from the church to the courtyard to preside over the simple grave dug to receive Faith's earthly body.

There was an empty space in the hearts of the church members with the cat's passing. But there was joy, too, because there was not a thread of doubt that their faithful feline would be running hard for all eternity, chasing any errant mice out of Heaven's pearly gates.

Someday they'd all meet up again.

~⚬X⚬~

And a Little One Shall Lead Them

Nothing is so strong as real gentleness; nothing is so gentle as real strength.

–St. Francis de Sales, Roman Catholic saint

PRAIRIE WINTERS ARE TYPICALLY cold in Canada, but the full force of the season doesn't usually hit until the calendar turns, and residents trade in the festivities of the Christmas season for the January and February doldrums. Average temperatures in the Edmonton region of Alberta for the month of December are somewhere around –10° C (13° F).

However, conditions were considerably cooler in December 2009.

By mid-month, long-standing, historic cold weather records were being broken. On December 13, Environment Canada recorded a bone-crackling −46.1° C (−51° F) at the Edmonton International Airport, and if you add consideration for the wind chill, that temperature plummeted further to −58.4° C (−73.12° F).

Taking the Chill Out

It wasn't uncommon for the Sjogren family of Wetaskiwin, Alberta, to take the edge off winter by lighting their fireplace. The weather office forecasted a cold weekend, and so the Sjogrens stocked up on their firewood and planned a few quiet days at home.

Cold weather or not, Monday came as it always does, and by 6:00 AM, Martin Sjogren was on his way to work. His wife, Phyllis, had already woken up once before, at around three in the morning. Noticing the fire must have gone out and the house was cold, Phyllis turned up the furnace and returned to bed. But by 6:30 she woke again, upon hearing what she'd later call a "terrible sequence of yowls," despite the earplugs she usually wore. It appeared that the family's cat, an orange ball of fluff called Gepetto, was kicking up quite the fuss. It was unusual behavior for the typically genteel and agreeable cat who didn't usually say much, so Phyllis pried herself from underneath her warm covers to check it out.

As Phyllis sat up, she noticed the headache she'd been trying to get rid of for the last few hours was much worse, and that she was now nauseous as well. Dizzy and feeling increasingly ill, Phyllis forced her way to Gepetto, who was sitting at the top of the basement stairs. She bent over and gave him a few loving strokes in an effort to calm him down. It appeared to work, and in a few moments, Gepetto scooted down the stairs, and Phyllis started back to her bedroom. But she was sick, sicker than she ever remembered being, and so she called her husband at work and let him know how she was feeling.

Reflecting back, Martin realized some of Phyllis' symptoms were similar to ones he'd been experiencing that morning, and it got him thinking that there might be a problem in the house. Martin insisted Phyllis leave their home. He then called a family friend who worked with the gas company for help.

As it turned out, Gepetto's persistent howling was a godsend to the Sjogrens. Emergency personnel confirmed that there was a gas leak in the house. In fact, they estimated about 70 percent of the home was saturated with deadly carbon monoxide. Had Gepetto not persisted in his complaints, his mistress, who was diagnosed as being in stage-two carbon monoxide poisoning, would have most likely succumbed to the invisible and odorless fumes.

It took seven hours of oxygen therapy to help
Phyllis recover from her ordeal. Without her hero cat,
who was inducted into the 2009 Purina Animal
Hall of Fame, Phyllis would not have had the
opportunity to recover.

Other Critters We Love

Animals often strike us as passionate machines.

—Eric Hoffer, American philosopher

Horsing Around Is Good for the Soul

Piglet sidled up to Pooh from behind. "Pooh!" he whispered.

"Yes, Piglet?"

"Nothing," said Piglet, taking Pooh's paw. "I just wanted to be sure of you."

—A.A. Milne, author

THE BOND BETWEEN ANIMALS AND humans, and the healing potential that bond can forge, is something health care researchers have been studying for years. Dogs have been used as assistance dogs for the blind, the hearing impaired and even with individuals who have mobility challenges. Dogs have been used as pet therapy animals, visiting hospitals, senior centers and other institutional living environments. They have also provided special companionship to youth who struggle with abuse issues or have learning disabilities.

Animals in general have a calming effect on humans, giving the people they work with the sense that they are loved or cared for unconditionally. So it's not surprising that the role of therapy animal isn't something that's reserved for dogs alone. Something as simple as fish tanks stocked with colorful exotic varieties or bird cages with parrots or canaries is as commonplace in seniors' homes across North America as the favorite cat hopping up on an individual's lap—these simple actions provide the seniors with a measure of comfort and calm.

Even a skeptic, or someone who isn't fond of animals, can see the value in this kind of interchange. Although these animals require care and, in the case of higher performing service animals such seeing-eye dogs, specialized training, they're generally small creatures and easily contained.

Well, most of them are.

The First of a New Generation

The Ismael Pinto Equine Therapy Centre is a non-profit association in Madrid, Spain, founded in 2002 and made up of health professionals and researchers who develop programs of treatment for people who can benefit from horse therapy. The centre also provides education and training for individuals interested in implementing this kind of therapy. Innovative, certainly, but although the centre is a leader in its field, it's certainly not the first program of its kind.

In the information it provides visitors to its website, the centre credits the Greeks with recognizing the therapeutic benefits of the horse as far back as 460 BC, with the ancient Greek physician Hippocrates highlighting the benefits of horseback riding on the mind and body. Official studies on the theory and therapy began in 1875, with French neurologist Charles Marie Edouard Chassaignac suggesting that "a horse in action improved the balance, motion and control muscle of his patients." The movement and subsequent rhythmic motion of riding on horseback seemed to offer something different for patients taking part in this activity as compared with other animal therapy options. The therapy is a bit about touch and feel—as Piglet suggested to Pooh, it was about being sure of something.

Continued studies over the last century have cemented the belief that working with and riding horses can prove therapeutic in many situations. As it's become more and more prominent over recent years, equine therapy has been used successfully for people with autism, hearing impairment, asthma, communication problems, emotional disorders, Down's syndrome, cerebral palsy, amputations, cardiovascular deficiencies and visual impairment.

New Program, New Focus

It all started when Vietnam veteran John Nash became haunted by nightmares and flashbacks to his combat experiences. The feelings of doom he struggled with challenged his abilities to cope with daily life, and before long he was self-medicating with alcohol and swimming in depression.

Medication and therapy helped to an extent, but Nash still found himself wandering about his farm and inevitably making his way to the horse barn. Some days he'd just curl up on the hay and fall asleep, and just to let him know he wasn't alone, his horse, Rain, would nuzzle him gently. Nash may not have immediately recognized the calming effect Rain had on him, but over time, the man understood that he needed to go to the barn, needed to be close to Rain. Nash knew the horse filled him with a kind of peace and contentment he couldn't get anywhere else, and he felt something inside him change. He had come to understand that he had developed a connection to the animal that went deeper than it had before. Rain's simple actions weren't just something the horse did by rote. Rain could sense when the man was depressed, and she responded with a kind gesture; in Nash's mind, this translated into obvious concern for the man's well-being. In his own words, he began to recognize "the power of the horse."

Nash testifies how Rain, with her gentle persistence and unconditional love, gave him his life back at a time when he was about ready to give up; Rain was nothing less than Nash's hero. The horse's natural behaviors set the foundation for an idea that came to Nash. He reasoned that if the horse was a therapeutic animal for him, the same could be true for other war veterans.

Because he was familiar with horses, having grown up with the animals, it only made sense that he acquired his certification as an equine specialist. From there it was a leap, but a very doable leap, to developing a specialized program that related to the demographic Nash was targeting, and in February 2008, the Combat Veterans Cowboy Up program was founded at the Moon Fall Ranch, just outside of Colorado.

Programs like the one Nash established have served in other parts of the United States in recent years. Brave Hearts Therapeutic Riding & Educational Center has been running in McHenry County, Illinois, since 1993, and the center's Veterans Program was founded in July 2007. The 7 Star Therapeutic Riding Center in Amarillo, Texas, is another equine therapy location offering services to veterans, especially those returning from Iraq and Afghanistan.

As animal therapists continue to embrace the horse in their programs and develop new ways to use the animal, more stables are being established across North America. For war veterans like Nash who have experienced the healing power the horse can provide, you can't have enough of them.

Part Three

ABOVE AND BEYOND

The only way to discover the limits of the possible is to go beyond them into the impossible.

–Arthur C. Clarke, British science-fiction author and inventor

EVER THINK YOU COULD LIFT A CAR with your bare hands? Maybe jump from a second-story window with a baby in your arms and both survive the fall? Or perhaps manage to tackle a would-be robber grabbing an elderly woman's purse? These are just a couple of the scenarios spelled out in stories of human heroism throughout the years. The folks we call heroes often don't recall making a conscious choice to do the things they did. In many instances, the "fight or flight response" takes over, pumping our bodies with adrenalin and giving us the strength and the courage to accomplish what should be impossible.

Animals faced with similar situations, where an instantaneous reaction is necessary for survival, seem to kick it into high gear as well. Of course, animals and humans alike can choose to flee a dangerous situation, rather than face it head on. We might not hear about them as much as we hear about war and pestilence and earthquakes and other tragedies, but our world is full of heroes who don't flee. Instead, these people face off against what looks to be impossible odds, and they manage to overcome great obstacles in the process.

The stories that follow focus on pets that have done the very same thing. Instead of running away from a desperate situation and worrying about their own safety, these animal companions have withstood potentially life-threatening events to protect and serve their masters.

Dogs, Dogs, Dogs

A dog is the only thing on earth that loves you more than he loves himself.

–Josh Billings, American humorist

Who's Your Mama?

My family doesn't share genes, we share love.

–Valerie Harper, actress and adoptive mother

USUALLY THE BIG HEADLINES surrounding a house fire revolve around a family being left homeless. If any children are involved, they are certain to make the news. But despite the fact that a house fire in Melbourne, Australia, affected five children in a family of seven, it was some of the family's four-legged pets that were catapulted onto the headlines.

While the cause of the fire that occurred at the Pilgrim St. Seddon home on October 26, 2008, wasn't clear, reports published in *The Daily Telegraph* and the *Herald Sun* uniformly saluted an 11-month-old terrier named Leo as the unlikely hero of the story. The drama began sometime around 9:00 PM. Janine Kelly was home with three of her children, 18-year-old Paul, 11-year-old Tayla and five-year-old Jayme, when the fire broke out at the front of the house. Janine and the children didn't realize a fire was brewing until someone ran to the back of the house and started yelling at them to get out. It was later discovered that the family's smoke detectors weren't working, so it was fortunate that neighbors noticed the blaze.

The Kellys' 43-year-old neighbor, Rob Easterbrook, knew that children were in the house. His first concern was to make sure they had all escaped unharmed before he tried to put out some of the flames that were being fueled by garbage on the family's front veranda. While neighbors were helping where they could, Tayla rushed back into the house to try to rescue some of the family's pets. She managed to find Barney, one of the Kellys' two dogs, but the other dog Leo was still trapped inside, as was Sabrina, a mother cat, and her litter of kittens. Tayla could see Leo standing over the kittens, but she couldn't get to him because of the fire.

By then, firefighters had arrived on the scene and cordoned off the area to prevent anyone else from trying to return to the burning building. The Kelly children were frantic about their missing pets. It was clear at this point that the smoke and flames had overcome the building, and the only people qualified and equipped to take another stab at retrieving the pets were the firefighters on the scene.

Fire officials were a little leery to risk their lives in an attempt to find animals they thought were likely dead, but to appease the stressed children, they made the attempt anyway. While medical personnel attended to the family's needs, one brave officer entered the house. After a quick look around, he discovered Leo stretched out on the floor beside the litter of kittens. It appears that while Sabrina had panicked and rushed to safety, young Leo felt compelled to protect the cat's four helpless babes.

"The dog had remained stoically guarding the box of kittens, even though their mother had disappeared," Ken Brown, the western zone commander from the Metropolitan Fire and Emergency Services Board (MFB) told reporters. "Leo wouldn't leave the kittens, and it nearly cost him his life."

When he was found, apparently Leo was listless, barely breathing and nearly unconscious, but he wouldn't willingly leave the kittens. The unnamed firefighter, who had to carefully sidestep downed power lines resulting from the fire, had to scoop the terrier up into his arms and rush him outside. The man's colleagues worked to resuscitate the pup using a combination of oxygen and heart massage.

Surprisingly, firefighters were able to return to the building one more time to retrieve the box of kittens. By the time they'd carted the youngsters outside, Leo had revived somewhat. The first thing he did on seeing the kittens was bend over to lick them all, tail wagging the entire time.

Young Leo survived his ordeal, as did the four kittens he stood watch over and their mother, who turned up sometime after all the commotion had died down. Following the rescue, the firefighters nicknamed the pup "Smoky," while the media added such monikers to his repertoire as "Leo the Lion-hearted" or simply "Hero Dog."

Members of the MFB were so amazed by Leo's dedication that they nominated the terrier for the Royal Society for the Prevention of Cruelty to Animals' award for bravery.

To the Kelly family, however, no medal was necessary to announce Leo as a hero. They knew that from the beginning. Although they'd lost everything in the blaze, which caused an estimated $150,000 in damages, the family survived with their lives.

And thanks to Leo, so did the pets.

Bubba

No matter how little money and how few possessions you own, having a dog makes you rich.

—Louis Sabin, *All About Dogs As Pets*

IT'S BEEN SAID THAT THE ONLY thing constant in life is change, and change often brings with it suffering. For Saundra Frazer, a succession of life changes over a relatively short period spelled significant loss early in her life. In 2009, the 27-year-old's fiancé, Jimbo, had passed away, and in January 2010, the young woman lost her mother as well.

Experiencing such poignant despair would leave most of us struggling to find our way. Frazer was surely no exception. She had one thing to be grateful for—her trusty companion, an amber-colored seven-year-old golden retriever named Bubba. The dog once belonged to Jimbo, but since his passing, Saundra had become Bubba's mistress. It was a small comfort to have this bit of her fiancé close by.

Saundra was also hoping for a new start, somewhere other than Fort Lauderdale, Florida, the community the couple once called home. And so in early 2010, Saundra, along with her friends and former neighbors, Charles McCauley and his girlfriend, Lori, moved a little farther north, to Lake Worth.

On their arrival in Lake Worth, the friends settled into a home in the 200 block of North J Street. Charles and Lori moved into the back part of the house, and Saundra and Bubba primarily occupied the front portion. In the late evening hours of February 8, 2010, everyone in the home was asleep when Bubba started barking. According to several news reports, Bubba persisted for some time, prodding his mistress with his nose and barking until he managed to wake her. Charles and Lori, hearing all the noise Bubba was making, woke about the same time Saundra did, but by the time the couple rushed out of their bedroom to see what was going on, Saundra was already working hard to douse the rapidly spreading flames. Charles tried to help her, but it was quickly apparent that the fire was more than the trio could handle.

Charles' first concern was to get Lori, Saundra and the animals out of the house. Bubba was easy to find, but Stewie, the family's cat, seemed to have disappeared. Saundra was concerned with saving some treasured mementos of those loved ones who'd passed away and as many of her photographs as possible. Clutching what few singed items she could, Saundra finally left the house.

What was left of the home once firefighters put out the blaze was uninhabitable. With no place to live, no transportation with which to get around and no jobs at that point in their journey, Saundra and her friends were destitute.

In the midst of yet another crisis, Saundra, however, did have something to be grateful for, as did Lori and Charles. They were alive. Had it not been for Bubba's persistence in waking his mistress, all three residents might have been overcome by smoke inhalation long before the flames destroyed their home.

"He's a hero. If we didn't get out, [the fire] was going to overwhelm us," Charles told reporters from the *Palm Beach Post*. "He's a champ."

Firefighters investigating the blaze theorized that an electrical short might have started the fire, or perhaps Stewie had knocked over a candle Saundra had been burning earlier that evening. Whatever the cause, Saundra, Lori and Charles were left with nothing—but their lives.

And thanks to Bubba, Saundra also has a devoted and loving companion she will always know she can trust. Even with her life.

~※~

One Boy's Guardian Angel

…then no harm will befall you,
no disaster will come near your tent.
For he will command his angels concerning you
to guard you in all your ways;
they will lift you up in their hands,
so that you will not strike your foot against a stone.

—Psalm 91:10–12

CAUTIOUS. ELUSIVE. SO SECRETIVE are the mountain lions of British Columbia that even the most daring mountaineers or backcountry hikers would consider themselves extremely lucky should they ever catch a glimpse of one during their travels. And yet the animals are there—lurking in the distance, creeping nearby, watching every move you make.

But cougars, as these animals are also known, are curious creatures. They can follow a hiker far too close for comfort or roam about, watching what's going on from a distance. This isn't usually a cause for concern. The shy, phantom-like loner doesn't normally associate with others of its own species, never mind purposefully making itself known to a human. This behavior is one of the reasons why Native Americans nicknamed the cougar the "shadow, or ghost, cat."

For the most part, cougars live within a self-determined geographic area that they will defend fiercely if necessary. The only time the animals mingle with other cougars is during mating season, and mothers, of course, stay close by their cubs until they're ready to venture off on their own.

This animal's love for anonymity makes the wilds of British Columbia a prime habitat. With 95 percent of the province being made up of Crown land, these feral cats can roam undetected and undisturbed within a fairly large area and don't usually come into close contact with family pets. It's a good thing too. In 1991, the BC Wildlife Branch estimated that about 3000 cougars live in the province. And since an adult male cougar needs a range of about 58 square miles, and a female needs about a third of that amount, it's a plus for this animal that urban sprawl hasn't overly taxed their habitat.

Another plus for cougars living in British Columbia is the abundance of ungulates and other wildlife species available to appease their carnivorous diets—an adult male cougar can easily consume as many as 20 mule deer in a year. That same average adult male cougar can weigh about 125 pounds, although some specimens have weighed as much as 210 pounds. Cougars are fast, strong and can down a 595-pound moose. With an ample supply of deer, moose, elk and other game animals in the province, it's uncommon for cougars to attack humans. Dogs and cats, even horses, are also usually safe from becoming a cougar's main course.

There are, of course, exceptions to this rule.

Everything Has a Weakness

An "Information Guide to Cougars in BC," published by the Internet site BritishColumbia.com, states that in the last 100 years, only five human deaths caused by wildlife were attributed to cougar attacks: four of those fatalities occurred on Vancouver Island. Another 29 non-fatal attacks were recorded during the same time period. Twenty of those took place on Vancouver Island, and most involved children younger than 16 years old. "In comparison, bees kill upwards of three Canadians every year," the site states.

Since cougar attacks in BC aren't usually because there's a food shortage for the big cats, it's been suggested that a child's unpredictable movements and their higher-pitched voices might confuse a cougar into thinking the youngster is actually a wild animal suitable for supper. It's unclear if this might have been the reason for a cougar attack in the Fraser Valley community of Boston Bar on January 2, 2010, but 11-year-old Austin Forman wasn't about to stand around and analyze the situation.

The incident, heralded by news agencies across North America, took place around 5:00 PM that Saturday as Austin was gathering firewood in his family's backyard. It was a chore he often did, and as the young boy was loading the wheelbarrow with firewood and getting ready to transport it from the woodpile to the house, he noticed his typically calm dog, Angel, frantically yipping and barking.

Although Austin thought Angel's behavior strange, he wasn't overly concerned about it. Perhaps the 18-month-old golden retriever noticed a rodent or saw a deer in the distance. While Angel became more and more animated, Austin continued with his chores. Soon the boy was pushing the wheelbarrow toward his family's home when Angel suddenly rushed toward the boy in an effort to protect him from another animal leaping in Austin's direction. Initially, the boy was a bit flustered by Angel's actions and wasn't sure what had just happened. On seeing Angel and another animal in some kind of skirmish, Austin thought the dog might have become embroiled in an unprovoked dogfight. But when the charging animal, which to that point Austin hadn't identified, chased Angel under the porch, the backlight gave the boy a clear view of what his pet was dealing with. "I knew at that moment, I had to go inside," Austin later told CTV BC News.

The unthinkable had just occurred—a cougar had attacked Austin.

Angel, aware of the imminent attack long before it occurred, had jumped between the cougar and Austin in an effort to distract the big cat and lure him away from the boy. Although the dog was successful in diverting the cougar's attention from its original target, and Austin was safe in the house, Angel was in big trouble.

If Austin and his mother, Sherrie, didn't move quickly, Angel wouldn't survive.

"9-1-1. What's Your Emergency?"

It took mere seconds, but it felt like time slowed for Austin and his mother. As Austin frantically relayed what had happened, telling his mom that their pet was being eaten by a cougar, Sherri grabbed the telephone and first dialed her father-in-law's number and then 9-1-1. As Sherri was telling the operator about the cougar attack, Angel's snarls and barks were turning into whines and yelps. The dog had rushed under the back porch and was burying her head in the corner, trying to protect herself as best she could. The cougar had complete control of the situation, though. If help didn't arrive in record time, the big cat's persistence might soon pay off with Angel becoming its dinner.

While Sherri was telling the operator about the danger underneath her porch, the operator was contacting Boston Bar RCMP Constable Chad Gravelle. The officer was finishing off the day's paperwork when the call came through that there was a cougar attack a half mile away. In a small town with a population of only about 900, that kind of call is immediately disconcerting. Chances were pretty good that Gravelle knew the people involved, and when he heard the attack was at the Formans' home, his guess was confirmed—he indeed knew the family.

Gravelle ran out the door and into his squad car, and within minutes, he was in the Formans' backyard, edging his way to the now muffled sounds coming from underneath the family's back porch. "I could see the cougar had the dog in its mouth, around the dog's neck. It was chewing on its neck," Gravelle told Canwest News Service reporter Lora Grindlay.

With his flashlight in one hand and his semi-automatic pistol in the other, Gravelle raised his gun and pulled the trigger once, then again. The bullets hit the cougar's behind. But an injured cougar is a desperate cougar, and desperation breeds panic. If Gravelle didn't get away another clean shot, he could become the big cat's next target. While the cougar continued to attack Angel, Gravelle moved a little closer, keeping his shooting arm steady. Once he got to within a couple of yards of the cougar and Angel, Gravelle fired again. There was no need for another blast. The bullet from Gravelle's third shot lodged in the cougar's head.

Austin's cousin, Travis Conkin, happened to be at the Forman home that day, and after the shots were fired, Conkin ventured outside. All Conkin and Gravelle could see underneath the porch was a ball of fur. Neither animal was moving.

Conkin approached the inanimate ball of fluff and pulled the cougar, which still had his mouth around Angel's head, off the lifeless dog. Angel remained motionless. Gravelle and Conkin held their breath. They could have heard a pin drop in the snow, but they couldn't hear Angel breathing. And then, just when they'd given up all hope, Angel gasped and, with blood dripping from her mouth, started taking rough, throaty breaths. It was sheer love and concern that compelled the wounded Angel to drag her injured body through the snow and to Austin's side following the attack—it appeared that the dog was anxious to see if Austin was okay. Surprisingly, Angel was still alive.

But would she stay that way?

A Two-Hero Day

With the nearest veterinary hospital located in Chilliwack, about 73 miles away, the Formans weren't able to get their hero-dog to a veterinarian until Monday. While the Formans worked to calm Angel and make her as comfortable as they could, the situation made for an anxiety-filled weekend. It was clear that the pup had several puncture wounds around her head, and her golden coat was covered in blood. No one had any clue what the extent of her injuries might include, but everyone was hopeful that she'd survive.

Once Angel finally arrived at the Sardis Animal Hospital, it was clear she was luckier than anyone might have imagined. The cougar's powerful jaw had fractured the dog's skull, and Angel had several puncture wounds around her face and head, as well as several less critical injuries to the rest of her body. Somehow she had miraculously avoided Gravelle's bullets.

Angel underwent an hour and a half of reconstructive surgery so veterinarians could repair the damage, but the family was optimistic. The Formans were told their beloved pet had a good chance of making a full recovery.

"If the cougar's tooth had gone another three-eighths of an inch back, it would have penetrated the brain case," Dr. Jack Anvik told Jennifer Feinberg of the *Chilliwack Progress*. "[Angel] is recovering incredibly well."

Angel spent a few days at the animal hospital and was then transported to the home of one of the Formans' friends in an effort to prevent her from getting too excited over seeing Austin and his sister, Holly, before she was well enough. But Angel was back to her old self in no time.

Of course, Angel owed any hope of living a long life to Constable Gravelle. Were it not for his quick response and keen marksmanship, the story might have had a tragic outcome. Gravelle received a medal for his efforts and, in turn, he and his wife decided to name the baby boy they were expecting, Austin.

One Smart Dog

Angel's story "went viral," as the *Chilliwack Progress* suggested, drawing the interest of news agencies across the continent, with the media conglomerates of CNN, NBC, CBS and Fox networks, as well as the American news show *Inside Edition*, airing the story. Angel's story warmed the hearts of viewers everywhere.

And if you analyzed Angel's interaction with the cougar, it was remarkable how the dog's instinct directed her to handle the situation the best way possible. According to all the best advice on how to deal with a cougar confrontation, Angel did everything correctly. She didn't back down or show any weakness. She barked with all her might, making it quite obvious she wanted to protect Austin from the cougar and at the same time warn him of the impending danger. And she fought back in the smartest way possible—by protecting her most vulnerable body parts.

In the end though, the most important part of that entire day was that Austin was safe and sound.

To reward his dog's efforts, Austin has vowed his undying love—and a steak dinner.

Paying It Forward

No kind action ever stops with itself. One kind action leads to another. Good example is followed. A single act of kindness throws out roots in all directions and the roots spring up and make new trees. The greatest work that kindness does to others is that it makes them kind themselves.

–Amelia Mary Earhart, American author and
aviation pioneer

DID YOU KNOW THAT IN THE United States on any given day, as many as 70,000 puppies and kittens are born? About one million of those puppies are placed in shelters throughout the year because the dog owners who allowed their pet to have a litter didn't take the time to find homes for the puppies.

Of course, shelters don't just deal in puppies. Individuals or animal control personnel collect another 3.5 million stray animals that make their way to shelters throughout the U.S. in any given year. Pet owners are responsible for surrendering another one million animals to be euthanized, and another two million are family pets that are placed in shelters for adoption.

Staggering figures to be sure, but what's even more disturbing is that of those animals, somewhere between four and six million are euthanized in any given year because no suitable adoptive homes are found for these innocent creatures.

And while the numbers aren't quite as high in Canada, they are still mind boggling, with an estimated 220,000 cats and dogs being surrendered or captured and taken to shelters every year, and around 80,000 of those animals are euthanized.

Given those statistics, the odds didn't look very good when a chow chow named Jarod landed himself in a shelter in Genelle, British Columbia, in the summer of 2006. Because everyone wants a puppy, puppies are usually the first to be adopted: Jarod was not a puppy.

He did stand out from other potential adoptees, however. He was a chow chow, and because unique breeds usually attract a lot of attention, there was a pretty good chance someone might adopt him between the time of Jarod's capture and the maximum number of days an animal is kept at some shelters before they are euthanized.

On the other hand, a chow chow requires a certain kind of dog owner. The dog's coat is thick and heavy and needs quite a lot of maintenance. And although the breed has a reputation for being extremely loyal and protective, it can also be timid and sometimes be picky when it comes to socializing with other pets or people outside the dog's immediate family.

Clearly, Jarod would have to turn up the charm if he were to manage and attract himself a new home.

Lucky Break

Donna Perrault loved chow chows, and as luck would have it, she'd been surfing the Internet and came across an "urgent listing" posted on the Northwest Chow Rescue of Oregon website. There was Jarod, a beautiful black chow chow, in desperate need of a home or he was facing an end to a relatively short life. One look at seven-year-old Jarod's photograph and Perrault knew what she had to do next. She adopted Jarod.

Perrault already owned a chow chow, a 12-year-old cinnamon variety named Meesha, and it wasn't long before the two dogs became friends. In October 2007, Perrault learned just how dear she and Meesha had become to Jarod.

The day began innocently enough, and as the afternoon light began to dim, the evening looked appropriately serene. Perrault was on the telephone talking with her son while Meesha nestled outside near the family's truck enjoying a little fresh air. Jarod was curled up inside the house. It was at this time that Perrault heard Meesha kicking up a fuss.

Perrault could tell by the tone in Meesha's bark that something was definitely wrong, and when she turned to look outside her window, she saw a large bear rushing toward Meesha. And although

Meesha was elderly and frail, she wasn't about to back down without a fight.

Without a second thought, Perrault dropped the telephone and ran outside, yelling at the bear and throwing a bucket at the raging animal. The bear turned and swatted his mammoth paws in the air toward Perrault's chest. By this time, Perrault realized that Jarod had managed to push the door open and had made his way outside, too. Jarod was barking ferociously and snapping at the bear's backside, eventually getting the bear's attention on himself instead of Perrault.

With the bear's focus now on Jarod, Perrault grabbed what she thought was a shovel or pitchfork but was actually a simple kitchen mop. Perrault swatted at the bear, hoping to get it away from her beloved dogs, and at one point she managed to hit the bear in the nose. One would have thought that all the commotion caused by Perrault's screams, Jarod's nipping and Meesha's barking should have frightened the bear off, but this was a persistent critter. If anything, the opposition to its presence only served to agitate the bear further.

Perhaps the bear considered Jarod the most annoying of the bunch because at one point it turned and started to chase the dog around the house. This gave Perrault enough time to unleash Meesha and take her into the house. Perrault now had to refocus her attention on Jarod and the threatening bear outside. In the meantime, Jarod was already rushing her way and bolted inside. Perrault thankfully latched the door behind him. The bear, apparently tired from the entire altercation, wasn't anywhere to be found.

Now that they were all safe, Perrault returned to the telephone to assure her son—who'd been on the line the entire time and had listened with great concern to the chaos—that all was okay. She also had a chance to examine the dogs and herself for any injuries. Although Meesha had been tossed about by the bear and was covered in saliva, the aging chow hadn't sustained any serious wounds. Jarod had received a single puncture wound to his back but otherwise was okay. And, looking down at her chest, Perrault noticed a long scratch across her chest.

While it's not uncommon for bears to wander near British Columbia's rural communities, and every now and again come into contact with people, these animals don't usually behave as aggressively as the bear did on that day. Thankfully, Jarod was on hand to smartly distract the large carnivore and, in the process, protect the woman who saved his life as well as a canine companion he'd come to love.

Undoubtedly, Jarod's biggest reward for his self-less bravery was that his family unit remained intact, and there wouldn't be another shelter experience in Jarod's near future. But for Perrault and her family and friends, their undying appreciation simply wasn't enough.

To that end, Jarod was officially recognized for his actions with the BC SPCA's 2008 Animal Hero Award. He was also inducted into the Purina Animal Hall of Fame in 2009.

Get Help, Buddy

If you want loyalty—get a dog. If you want loyalty and attention—get a smart dog.

—Grant Fairley, motivational speaker

WILLOW, ALASKA, WAS FIRST SETTLED in 1897 when an influx of miners moved into the area to dig for gold. Today, the community has a population of about 1658, but many of the families live scattered throughout the more than 75 miles of backcountry roads. It's the rustic, earthy quality of life that attracts folks who value their privacy and enjoy living in an area where the human footprint is minimal, and for the most part, they like to keep it that way.

At the same time, living in the wilderness has its drawbacks. And on the evening of April 4, 2010, 23-year-old Ben Heinrichs was about to experience one of those drawbacks.

That night, Heinrichs was in his workshop situated beside his family's Caswell Lakes home. Even though it was officially spring, the night was cold and a blanket of snow still covered the ground. In order to keep warm, Heinrichs had the heater on as he worked away on parts for his truck. His German shepherd, Buddy, was curled up nearby.

All in all, it was a peaceful, wintry scene, until the heater ignited either some chemicals or gasoline, starting a fire that caught on some of Heinrichs' clothes. As Heinrichs rushed outside to roll in the snow, the flames rapidly began to overtake the shed. Despite his anxiety, Heinrichs had the presence of mind to shut the shed door behind him to prevent the fire from spreading. However, he realized that in so doing, he had trapped Buddy in a burning inferno. Rushing back to the shed, and still on fire, Heinrichs called the dog and, as Buddy ran out of the building, Heinrichs was close behind.

"I just took off running," Heinrichs told Rachel D'Oro of the Associated Press. "I said we need to get help, and he just took off."

At first, Heinrichs thought the dog was disappearing into the woods out of fear. Buddy was running, but not into the woods. Instead, he bolted down the road and onto Caswell Loop Road where Alaska State Trooper Terrence Shanigan was driving in search of the Heinrichs' home. He was responding to an emergency call placed by Heinrichs' neighbor who'd noticed the fire. Shanigan was on the line with dispatch trying to locate the burning house and was frustrated with the process because his car's GPS wasn't working. It was at that moment that he came face to face with a dog running toward him.

A video clip from the officer's patrol car revealed what happened next. It appeared that Buddy, on seeing the patrol car, recognized it as an emergency vehicle of some type and immediately turned back toward his master's home. The police officer, going on instinct and believing the dog was somehow connected to the family in trouble, turned to follow.

"He wasn't running from me, but was leading me," Shanigan later told reporters. "I just felt like I was being led…it's just one of those things that we're thinking on the same page for that brief moment."

Running at top speed, and slowing only enough for a quick shoulder check every so often to ensure the patrol car was still behind him, Buddy made it back to the Heinrichs' property in record time. By now, the shop was completely engulfed in flames, with tongues of fire leaping from the shed and stretching into the night sky, threatening both nearby trees and other buildings, including the Heinrichs' home.

But Buddy had done his job. He got help. After greeting Shanigan as he got out of the car and nudging the officer toward the fire, Buddy took off again. It seemed as though the shy dog had had quite enough excitement for the day and disappeared until things quieted down.

By the time the fire trucks arrived, the shop was pretty much flattened, and a nearby wood shed was also heavily damaged, but firefighters doused the flames before they spread to the house. Aside from some damage around the kitchen window, the family home had been spared.

In a press release issued by Alaska State Trooper Director Colonel Audie Holloway, Buddy's efforts were praised as the catalyst that prevented an already disastrous situation from becoming catastrophic. "Buddy's valiant actions saved Trooper Shanigan valuable time in responding to the fire... Buddy's pluckiness is a bright spot among an otherwise tragic event for the Heinrichs family."

Although Ben and his parents, Lynnette and Thomas Heinrichs, were immensely grateful to Buddy for his amazing actions, and well aware that their family pet was a hero, that wasn't enough for the Alaska State Troopers. And on April 23, less than a month after the fire, the department formally recognized Buddy for his heroic actions. To mark the occasion, the German shepherd was presented with a large rawhide bone and an engraved, stainless steel bowl, and the Heinrichs family was given a framed letter telling of Buddy's efforts.

"He's my hero," Ben said, giving Buddy a pat with his still bandaged hands.

It's not the first time Buddy intervened to help his people. On two separate occasions the pup, born to a mother who'd served as a canine officer, chased a bear away from Ben during a fishing excursion. This time, though, Thomas suggested that Buddy must have had a little divine intervention.

Either way, there's no doubt that Buddy will live out his days lavished with love and appreciation, and that he will continue to protect the family he adores.

~∞∞~

Tag-team Duo

The ordinary man is involved in action, the hero acts. An immense difference.

–Henry Miller, American author

THIS TALE, WHICH COMES OUT OF Newark, New Jersey, took place early on the morning of July 31, 2009. Around 1:30 AM, long before anyone was ready to wake, the Arrington family dog started fussing. Smoke, a pit bull likely named for his charcoal-gray coat, started nibbling on 10-year-old Jose Colon-Arrington's ear. Smoke, desperate to rouse his master, continued to lick and nudge the boy until Jose finally awoke to a haze of smoke.

The quick-thinking youngster, recognizing the urgency of the situation, ran through the upstairs bedrooms looking for any family members who might be asleep. Finding all the rooms empty, he ran downstairs and discovered his older sister, Kaity, sleeping on the couch. Unable to arouse his sister,

Jose dragged her to the front door where an alert neighbor who'd noticed the fire met him. Firefighters rushed in to combat the blaze just as Jose, Kaity and Smoke were led to safety.

As it turned out, the timing of the Arringtons' escape and the arrival of the fire department couldn't have been better. The grease fire responsible for the destruction was on the verge of spreading like wildfire.

The Arrington family had Smoke to thank for the happy ending to this story. While Jose did everything in his power to help his sister and make sure no other family members were in danger, had it not been for the persistence of Smoke, the brother and sister would quite likely have died in their sleep.

Interestingly enough, Lisa had allowed Smoke into the family quite begrudgingly. When the dog was adopted a year earlier, she had reservations about owning a pit bull. But Jose and his older brother, Samuel, fought for their choice of pet. Lisa told reporters she was very glad she relented, and Smoke became a part of their family.

It just goes to show you that nothing beats the power of a boy and his dog.

Heroic Love

It is surmounting difficulties that makes heroes.

–Louis Pasteur, French chemist and biologist

HEROISM, LIKE ANY OTHER VIRTUE, means different things to different people. Some of the most heroic people I've ever known never risked life and limb in order to accomplish some potentially deadly feat. Instead, they were the kind of people who put their love into action. They show their loyalty by standing by the people they love, regardless the situation.

Animal heroes can be like that, too. Some of the most touching stories of pet heroism I've come across were all about love. They told of how these animals refused to sever their attachment to their people, even, in some cases, after their masters died.

In a fickle world where love is as dispensable as torn socks or worn-out jeans, it's humbling to see the kind of dedication and faithfulness the animal companions in the following stories have shown for their humans.

A love like this is heroism at its finest.

Home Is Where the Heart Is

One of the happiest sights in the world comes when a lost dog is reunited with a master he loves. You just haven't seen joy till you have seen that...

—Eldon Roark, columnist and author

THEY NEVER TAKE ANY VOWS. Their owners don't provide them with written expectations or legal contracts with fulfillment requirements. Nor do they get paid for their wholehearted devotion. But there has never been a more loyal subject, more dedicated friend, more committed companion than a person's pet.

Despite the usual disagreements that come along when any two creatures co-habit, a pet is long-suffering, will tolerate even the most annoying tendencies and will do almost anything to please its owner. Try to separate a pet from its owners, and chances are you'll find yourself up against an impossible battle to gain a trust that belongs to another.

The concept of what might happen should a family pet become separated from its master so intrigued Sheila Burnford that the writer penned her first, and potentially most successful novel, on the topic. *The Incredible Journey* was published in 1961 and later made into two Disney films (*The Incredible Journey*, 1963, and *Homeward Bound: The Incredible Journey*, 1993). The story tells of how three family pets, a dog and two cats, become separated from their masters and travel 300 miles through the rocky lakes and forests of northwestern Ontario,

Canada, to be reunited with their owners. The animals' demonstration of affection in the story is a form of gentle heroism that proves the emotional depth of their loyalty. It proves the theory that animals do indeed have emotions.

Of course, Burnford's tale is fictional, but stories of that kind of attachment are a lot more common than most of us might think.

A Winding Road Home

In the summer of 2007, Rocky was still growing into his personality. The German shepherd, adopted in 2005 by a Scotsman named Ibrahim Fawal, loved to ride along on his master's scooter and was said to be great with children. In fact, everybody who knew the two-year-old pup loved him.

Apparently, new acquaintances developed a rapid attachment to the dog, too; while the Fawal family was on vacation, the pup was abducted. Sources suggest the dog was eventually dumped by his abductors and wandered about until a family from Salerno, Italy, a community roughly 400 miles from the dog's first home, adopted him.

It appears that although Rocky might have found himself in a different living situation, his affections weren't transferred so easily, and his new adoptive family reported how the shepherd was a runner, escaping with the ease of Houdini. Once free, Rocky would run, Forrest Gump style, as if he was on a mission to return to his first owner. And then his current family, or someone who knew him, managed to capture the dog and return him home.

One day he finally disappeared, and his new family was unable to locate him. When he was eventually picked up, hobbling near the city of Pisa in January 2010, his paws were raw and blistered, and he was rail thin. Whoever found the dog took him to a veterinary hospital, which ended the animal's perceived nightmare. Finding a tattoo on the animal, the vet tracked down Rocky's original owners. Fawal was overjoyed, as was the pooch. Apparently, Rocky's wanderlust wasn't about being disobedient to his new family; it was all about finding the master he loved.

He was finally home—and he isn't inclined to run any longer.

Stranger Than Fiction

If you live to be 100, I hope I live to be 100 minus one day, so I never have to live without you.

–Winnie the Pooh, children's storybook character

MUSICIAN STEVE SOLEAS LEFT his home in New Mexico in February 2010 for a few weeks to visit friends and check out the music industry in New Orleans. It wasn't his plan to take his six-year-old Labrador-mix dog Charlie along for the ride. Charlie, on the other hand, had other thoughts on the matter. Just days after

Soleas left New Mexico, Charlie, unhappy at being left behind, disappeared. No one knew what had happened to the mutt; it was so unlike him to vanish.

If Soleas and his family thought it odd that Charlie bolted, they were about to have a harder time believing what came next. It appeared that Charlie had been discovered "running in the street" by a couple visiting near Taos, New Mexico. The couple, who asked the media that they remain anonymous, said they opened their car door and called out to the all-white, collarless dog. Charlie leapt into their car without much encouragement, and his rescuers tried everything they could to identify the dog's owner. Unsuccessful, they decided to cash in their plane tickets and return home to New Orleans by car so they could take the pup, which, coincidentally, they had named Charlie, with them.

It wasn't until the couple approached Teresa Gernon of the Magazine Street Animal Clinic to have the dog checked over that it was discovered Charlie was actually implanted with a microchip. That's how they tracked down Soleas, who at the time was visiting a mere 50 blocks away.

The whole experience, which took place over a distance of 1200 miles, resolved itself in a relatively short 10-day time frame. And even though the couple that had found Charlie was planning to adopt him, they were thrilled to know the dog had been reunited with his rightful owner.

News reports credited Charlie with "hitchhiking" the 1200 miles separating him from his master. That might have been the dog's intention, but he no doubt thanked the universe for helping him out! Following Charlie's ordeal, man and dog enjoyed the next couple of weeks together in New Orleans. Soleas never had to worry about Charlie bolting again. The dog was exactly where he wanted to be.

~⊃✕⊂~

The Final Goodbye: Bobby and Sam

My grief lies all within. And these external manners of lament are merely shadows to the unseen grief that swells with silence in the tortured soul.

–William Shakespeare, writer

NO MATTER HOW DEDICATED animals are, or how all-encompassing their drive to find their master, sometimes a happy ending is not to be. The death of an animal owner, means that there is no hope for a reunion, at least not in this lifetime.

Of course, a dog might not know that.

The well-known story of Greyfriars Bobby has risen to legend status since it occurred in 1858. John Gray adopted the Skye terrier pup in 1856. The night watchman was looking for a companion as he patrolled the streets of Edinburgh, and Bobby, as he was called at that time, filled the role splendidly. But the happy partnership was a short-lived one. Stricken with tuberculosis, John passed away on February 15, 1858, just two years after adopting the pup. John was laid to rest at the Greyfriars Kirkyard in Edinburgh.

There wasn't any shortage of John's family and friends interested in adopting the terrier that now found himself an orphan, but Bobby would have none of these good intentions. Instead, he settled down by his master's graveyard and kept vigil. The scene saddened those who knew of Bobby's reluctance to leave his master's side, even in death, but most believed that in time Bobby would move on and claim another master.

Not so.

Dogged persistence by the cemetery's caretakers, who removed the dog on many occasions, couldn't prevent Bobby from returning to his master's side. It was clear the terrier wasn't going to move on any time soon, and since he was causing no harm, those same caretakers who finally stopped chasing him away built Bobby a small shelter beside John's grave. Day and night Bobby snuggled in the shelter. The only time he ventured away was at 1:00 PM, when he followed a local cabinetmaker named William Dow to a nearby coffee shop for his daily meal.

Bobby's loyalty won over the hearts of everyone who knew him, and they provided him with the ability to continue to serve his master, even after death.

One hurdle was cleared, but another was looming. In 1867, the city of Edinburgh passed a bylaw stating that all dogs required a license or they'd be impounded and destroyed. Of course, that meant that Bobby was facing a death sentence unless someone intervened on his behalf.

That's exactly what Sir William Chambers, the Lord Provost of Edinburgh, did. He paid for the dog's license and attached it to a special dog collar he'd had made, complete with the following brass inscription: "Greyfriars Bobby from the Lord Provost of Edinburgh 1867 licensed."

Bobby, who'd now acquired the moniker "Greyfriars Bobby," had overcome yet another roadblock. He continued to live by his master's side until Bobby died in January 1872, at the ripe old age of 16. He was buried in the same graveyard, a mere 75 yards from John's grave. A headstone was eventually erected at Bobby's grave, and in 1981, His Royal Highness the Duke of Gloucester CCVO unveiled the following inscription:

Greyfriars Bobby
Died 14th January 1872
Aged 16 years
Let his loyalty & devotion be a lesson to us all

The kind of faithfulness and devotion that the story of Greyfriars Bobby demonstrates still brings tears to the eyes of dog lovers more than 100 years later. It's the kind of good-news tale that, were it to happen today, the media would jump all over.

That's exactly what happened in April 2008.

Teddy Crockarell of Clarksville, Tennessee, succumbed to cancer on April 7, and it wasn't only his friends and family who were devastated by his death. According to Teddy's wife, Marcene, the man's 2½-year-old dachshund, Sam, knew something terrible had occurred as soon as his master died, and the dog disappeared almost immediately. Even though Sam wore an electric fence collar, making an attempt to cross the boundary surrounding his home quite painful for the little fellow, he simply vanished.

Although the family was struggling to come to terms with their grief over Teddy's death, they were now saddened by the loss of their pet. Ever since Sam came to live with the Crockarells as a new pup, he and Teddy had been inseparable. A bond that defies description was forged, and when Teddy died, something inside Sam appeared to break.

Despite their concern for their pet, the family continued to prepare for a funeral service. A few days later, while pulling up to the Community First Church of God on Trenton Road, a full six miles from the Crockarells' home, the family was shocked to see they had someone waiting for them. There, sitting near the front door to the church, was Sam.

"He was just shivering and sitting there by the doors," Marcene told reporters. "We just lost it, and all we were doing was hollering, 'Sam! Sam!' and here he comes and he was just all over all three of us."

Sam's trek had taken him across the very busy Wilma Rudolph Boulevard and into strange territory—Sam had never been to the church where Teddy's funeral was being held. What brought him there seemed nothing short of a miracle.

"This was God sent," Marcene told *ABC News*. "There was no other way that this little dog could come that far and never having been in the area at all."

Like the story of Greyfriars Bobby, it appeared as though not even death could separate dog from master. When Teddy's son-in-law, Howard, assessed the situation, it made perfect sense. "If he walked those six miles, he was looking for his papa...he found him."

Feisty Felines

True benevolence or compassion extends itself through the whole of existence and sympathizes with the distress of every creature capable of sensation.

–Joseph Addison, English essayist

That's Our Baby

I have studied many philosophers and many cats. The wisdom of cats is infinitely superior.

–Hippolyte Taine, French critic and historian

IF YOU'VE EVER BEEN PREGNANT OR in any way associated with a pregnant woman, you're probably well aware that by the time a woman has reached seven months gestation, she is starting to feel quite uncomfortable. In the last trimester, the mom-to-be is hauling around a much heavier belly, making daily activities harder to perform and a good night's rest more difficult to achieve. At this point in her journey, she's usually tired a good percentage of the time, and it's not uncommon for her to catnap when, after a long day, she finally gets the chance to put her feet up for a few minutes and relax.

That's exactly what happened to Letitia Kovalovsky on the evening of January 17, 2010. At the seventh-month mark of her pregnancy, the Chicago-area woman was tired and, because she was carrying twins, was even more uncomfortable. So when she and her boyfriend, Josh Ornberg, sat back to watch a little bit of Sunday night television, it wasn't long before Letitia fell asleep. Josh followed soon after.

As the clock ticked away and night turned into morning, the low rumble of the television competed with more than Josh and Letitia's gentle snores. Baby, the couple's 13-year-old cat, had been creating a ruckus for quite some time when, after her meows didn't get the attention the cat had hoped for, she pounced on the sleeping couple. The cat, who preferred her own company to anyone else's and would rather hide under the bed or in the bathtub than cuddle with her humans, had behaved so strangely that her actions managed to shock her owners out of their sleep.

Josh's first impressions were as murky as the room. Stunned by Baby's behavior, it took him a few seconds to clear his thoughts and focus his eyes. At first, Josh thought the lighting in the couple's living room seemed to be a different color. Soon he realized he was seeing everything through a haze of smoke. Uncertain what to make of the situation, Josh leapt from the couch and glanced down the hallway where he noticed what he later described to reporters as an "orange glow" coming from the vicinity of his bedroom.

Getting his girlfriend out of harm's way was Josh's first concern, and once he made sure Letitia was safely outside, as well as Blackjack, the couple's Bernese mountain dog, and Baby, Josh returned to the house. He ran to get the family's fire extinguisher and rushed down the hall to try to put out the fire that must have started during the night. Without any idea what awaited him, and unsure as to how a fire could have started in the couple's bedroom in the first place, he thrust open the bedroom door and started spraying. But it was clear the fire was far too established for Josh to contain it. He'd need some pretty large water-power if he had any hope of saving what remained of their home.

It took the Wonder Lake Fire Department only 30 minutes to contain the blaze, but by the time they were called in, the flames were already shooting "10 feet up in the air" according to assistant chief Mike Weber. Weber told PEOPLEPets.com that were it not for Baby's insistent prodding, which eventually woke Josh and Letitia, the fire could have consumed far more than parts of their house and contents—it could have cost the couple their lives. "She [Baby] was definitely the hero in this situation," Weber said.

When the final tally came in, Letitia and Josh had an estimated $68,000 in damages to a home they'd purchased just a few weeks earlier. Most of the contents in the home were damaged or destroyed by fire or smoke and water damage, and among those items were the cribs, clothes and other supplies the couple had purchased since Letitia discovered she was expecting.

There was one more loss to be recorded. Letitia and Josh knew Baby had bolted as soon as the front door had been opened, but when the smoke had cleared, it became clear that the cat who saved them from a certain death was nowhere to be found. Weber suggested the disappearance wasn't out of the ordinary because the fire might have spooked the cat into hiding. Baby likely would return once all the confusion subsided and the noisy fire trucks left, but the multicolored tabby's absence concerned Josh and Letitia nonetheless. After all, as Josh put it, the senior cat was their hero.

Determined to find their missing pet, Josh told the *Chicago Sun Times* that they set a trap near their home and baited it with Baby's favorite treat—tuna. Finally, after a two-day absence and with a belly grumbling for food, Baby was trapped. Back with her owners, the sometimes-standoffish cat now seemed a lot happier to be in the company of her people. "She was in the hotel jumping on the bed and playing," Josh told PEOPLEPets.com. "She has a different attitude now."

After the fire, it was clear that Josh and Letitia had a lot of rebuilding to do, but thanks to Baby, the couple had the chance to begin their new family with everyone present and accounted for.

~ঞ৫~

Always a Reason to Party

The cat seldom interferes with other people's rights. His intelligence keeps him from doing many of the fool things that complicate life.

—Carl Van Vechten, American writer

IN DECEMBER 2009, THE RUSSIAN newswire service RIA Novosti reported that a little too much vodka almost cost a man his life. On December 11, 2009, an unidentified man downed a few too many and passed out in his apartment, located in the Perm Territory in Russia's Urals. The cigarette he was smoking at the time fell and smoldered until it started a fire.

Luckily, the man lived with a cat that had a lot more sense than he did. As the smoke filled the small apartment, the cat began clawing at its master's face. Eventually, the persistent feline was able to wake the intoxicated man, who, surprisingly, managed to focus enough to call for help and then stumble to safety. By the time firefighters arrived, the apartment was engulfed in flames. Fortunately for other residents of the building, the only apartment damaged by the blaze was the one belonging to the tipsy tenant with the cat.

Looks like a lot of people called the kitty a hero that day.

Blame It on the Livestock

Earlier that year, and on the other side of the world, a couple was also thankful their feline friend had his wits about him when a fire broke out on their property. This time, however, the culprit wasn't a burning cigarette fallen from the mouth of an inebriated owner—it took firefighters a little longer to discover the cause of that blaze.

One night in January 2009, Jim and Kristi Giles of Warren County, Iowa, and their son John Hadley, were sleeping when John's cat woke its owner. Bleary-eyed and droopy with sleep, it took John a while before he cleared the cobwebs enough to notice his family's home was in flames. The man's first thought was to rush to his parents' bedroom to help his ailing mother and his father out of the burning building and into the frigid winter.

Firefighters were called to the blaze, but by the time they arrived, the home wasn't salvageable. Still, the family was safe and out of harm's way, and thanks to the cat's warning calls, John also managed to save the family's two goats and pet dog.

An investigation into the cause of the fire pointed to the inhabitants of the family's barn, which was attached to the house.

Firefighters surmised that one of the goats must have kicked over a space heater that had been placed in the barn for the animals to keep warm and that it had caused the fire.

~⌘~

The Conflagration

You will always be lucky if you know how to make friends with strange cats.

–Colonial proverb

ARTISTS ARE A STRANGE LOT. While most of the world favors the idea of working a nine-to-five job and sleeping through the night, it's not uncommon for more creative sorts to prefer working into those quiet, dark hours when the rest of the world is enjoying a good night's sleep.

Sandy Spreitz was just such an artist. As the last of the evening light faded and the sky darkened, Spreitz was on a roll. As his cat, Mo, was making her evening rounds, Spreitz was making great progress on the last part of a 700-page novel he'd been toiling over for some time, and he didn't want to turn in for the night until he dotted the end of his last sentence.

It was in the early morning hours of November 23, 2007, when Spreitz finally called it a day. There aren't many writers who complete an entire novel longhand before typing it into the computer these days, but Spreitz was one of those artists who still enjoyed the organic feel of a pen in the hand, the sound the nib makes on the blank page and the smell of the ink.

Spreitz was also quite proud of his book. He later told reporters from the *Oakland Tribune* that the tale revolved around a "tragic love story on an alien planet." He wasn't too pleased with his title, though he was hopeful that after a good night's sleep he'd be able to resolve that little detail. And so he tidied his workspace, tapping the four sides of his manuscript into a neat pile, turned out the lights and headed for bed.

Interrupted Sleep

It was about 5:00 AM when Mo started to get annoying. Spreitz had never really liked the irritating tabby. It's not that Spreitz wasn't a cat lover—he had enjoyed the companionship of another feline before Mo had come along and was just frustrated that his new pet couldn't hold a candle to her predecessor who, in Spreitz's mind, was a "prince of cats."

So when Mo started howling after Spreitz had just spent all his efforts and energy in his artistic endeavors a few hours earlier, he was more than a little peeved. If Mo wanted to start making a fuss, she could spend the rest of the night outside, Spreitz reasoned as he plopped the feline out the front door and returned to his warm bed.

The change in scenery didn't quiet Mo, though. The cat was still whining, and Spreitz could feel his blood pressure rising. Irked at all the noise, he jumped out of bed once again. Spreitz was starting to wonder if something was amiss, and if it wasn't, he would give Mo a piece of his mind. But when Spreitz opened his bedroom door, he noticed light flashing behind the pantry door—a light that wasn't supposed to be there. Turning his attention to the pantry, Spreitz grabbed the door handle and pulled it open.

What he discovered was beyond anything he could have ever imagined. Not only was his house on fire, but the beams of his cottage were also engulfed in large flames. There was nothing he could do but call 9-1-1, grab whatever he could carry—his keys, his boots, his cell phone—and rush out the door.

Spreitz phoned the fire department around 5:20, but the knowledge that firefighters would arrive shortly didn't appease him. Faced with the reality that he couldn't just stand there watching his house and the lifetime's worth of work it contained burn to the ground, Spreitz grabbed the garden hose and tried to hose down some of the flames. It was a valiant effort but a hopeless one. "I felt like a little boy peeing into Niagara Falls," Spreitz told reporters.

Trucks arrived at the scene shortly after the 9-1-1 call was made, and by 5:40 AM the flames were doused and the smoldering remains contained, but it was of small comfort to Spreitz. His home, a guesthouse built in the 1930s and nestled in an affluent, California community along Canyon Road, had sustained about $60,000 in damages.

It was insignificant, though, compared with a loss that for Spreitz was priceless. The book he'd been working on was nothing but a pile of ash, the MacBook he was going to type it into damaged beyond repair.

That was only the beginning.

The Momentous Loss

Spreitz's artwork collection included 10,000 pages worth of illustrations and paintings, dozens of handcrafted wooden puppets and six computers filled with his own musical compositions. He also lost a collection of rare books, many of which were early copies, and assorted vintage instruments. Spreitz couldn't begin to estimate the cost of the fire to his pocketbook and, more importantly, to him personally.

It could have been worse, though. Had it not been for his annoying cat, whose persistence didn't let up until she saw her master leave the burning building, Spreitz could have become another fatality.

Firefighters later surmised that either a faulty furnace or electrical problems caused the fire. Unfortunately, the two smoke detectors in the home weren't in working order, and so it was left to Mo to rouse the man from his fitful slumber. "Really, it if wasn't for that cat, [Spreitz] more than likely would have died in the fire," Ed Barton, Battalion Chief of Central County Fire Department told reporters.

Begrudgingly, Spreitz had to agree. He was still trying to process what had just occurred, as well as coming to terms with the loss of his artwork, but Spreitz conceded to reporters that although to that point Mo hadn't endeared herself to Spreitz, or to anyone else for that matter, he was grateful.

"She's still a bit of a bully..." he told reporters before adding, "Yeah, I love my Mo—and I'm still very glad she saved my life."

Mo disappeared for a while after the firefighters arrived, but she eventually returned, a little dazed by what she found. She may not have saved everything, but she sure saved her master who, thanks to the cranky cat, has a lifetime left to recreate and start anew.

For Mo's efforts, The Humane Society of the United States voted the cat as one of the top five animal heroes in the country.

Way to go, Mo!

Other Critters We Love

Lots of people talk to animals.... Not very many listen, though. That's the problem.

—Benjamin Hoff, *The Tao of Pooh*

Elephant Love

Be a good animal, true to your animal instincts.

—D.H. Lawrence, British writer

THERE'S SOMETHING MAGICAL in the air during the Christmas season. It doesn't matter if you're making snow angels and getting your face sprinkled with softly falling snowflakes in cooler climates or lounging on a tropical beach enjoying Mai Tais, the world seems to slow down a little. For a few days, peace on earth isn't just a dream; it's a possibility.

Even if keeping Christmas traditions isn't part of your routine, enjoying a few days away from work or taking a winter holiday is quite popular for many families.

And so it was that in 2004, eight-year-old Amber Mason (some sources state "Amber Owen") of Milton Keynes, England, was enjoying such a winter holiday with her mother and stepfather on the sandy beaches near Phuket, Thailand. Christmas Eve and Christmas Day were packed with the usual revelry. There were gifts to open and new toys to try out, but the typical North American festive turkey was replaced with a beachside barbecue dinner. As the Masons turned in for the night that Christmas, it was with full stomachs and warm hearts.

December 26 dawned bright and warm and promised yet another day of fun in the sun. Amber's parents, Samantha and Eddie, were recuperating from the busy festivities of the previous days. Amber was out on the beach playing with what was likely the best present she'd received that Christmas—the gift of a new, best friend.

Ning Nong wasn't any ordinary friend; he had extremely large ears, a long nose, cement-gray skin and weighed several hundred pounds: if you haven't guessed it by now, Amber's new friend was an elephant. Most of the holidaying youngsters were content to build sand castles and chase waves, but Amber was experiencing the adventure of a lifetime as she was toured along the shores of the Andaman Sea on the back of four-year-old Ning Nong, with his owner Yong nearby and keeping a close eye on the pair. Since her family's arrival in Phuket, the young girl and Yong's pet elephant had been inseparable. This was the best holiday ever. That morning, while Amber and Ning Nong were splashing in the waves, Yong was scooping up any fish unlucky enough to swim near the shallow waters of the shoreline and filling a basket for his hungry elephant's lunch. Suddenly, the waters began to recede, and more and more fish were flapping about on the sand. Yong, surprised at his good luck, kept catching the frantic fish, wandering a little farther in the direction of the sea. Amber, oblivious to any change in her environment, was enjoying her time with the young elephant.

Ning Nong, however, was starting to bristle a little. Amber was about to find out how very lucky she was to have befriended the young tusker.

The Middle of Nowhere

It wasn't supposed to happen. Major seismic events like earthquakes and their resulting tsunamis are considered rare occurrences in the Indian Ocean. But December 26, 2004, wasn't your typical day; that day the unthinkable happened.

According to the Thomson Reuters Foundation (the charitable branch of Thomson Reuters), an underwater event occurred off the west coast of Indonesia at 7:59 that morning, about 500 miles away from the seashore where Amber and Ning Nong were enjoying the sun.

In less than 10 minutes leading up to that moment, a shift had occurred that altered the structure of the earth's crust, sliding the Indian plate beneath the Burma plate, and putting into motion a succession of events that resulted in what the international media would eventually call the "largest magnitude earthquake in 40 years."

At first, this shifting of plates went unnoticed. The Indian Ocean, with an average depth of 11,150 feet, requires an event of cataclysmic proportions to move the volume of water the ocean holds. With swells as small as one foot in height spanning the open waters, even experienced sailors aren't always able to assess when the subtle rise and fall of the waves might indicate a potential tsunami. The scientists and seismic experts monitoring these types of events are relied on to warn sailing vessels and vacationers along nearby seashores of the impending danger.

Sadly, all too often, this silent killer lurks about unnoticed…until it's too late. News reports around the world highlighted the fact that no early-warning system was in place for such an occurrence in the Indian Ocean. So when the Christmas earthquake of 2004 shook the earth's core, measuring 9.15 on the Richter scale and sending shockwaves across the planet, no one was prepared.

There was scarcely a continent that wasn't affected in some way by the earthquake. Hailed as one of the largest earthquakes in history, it was said to have an impact equivalent to 23,000 Hiroshima-type bombs. The sheer force of it caused subsequent earthquakes as far away as Alaska. But it was the waves that caused the most carnage. Once the waters gained momentum, the waves were said to have washed as far as two miles inland in some parts of India,

Indonesia and Thailand. A shocking 13 countries bordering the earthquake zone were affected by the resulting tsunami, and 226,000 people died—166,000 in Indonesia alone. Another two million people were left homeless, and more than $14 billion in foreign aid was donated to help rebuild the devastated areas in the years following the event.

At the time, unbeknownst to the Masons, or anyone else holidaying in Phuket, the island was in the direct path of Mother Nature's fury.

The Calm Before the Storm

Yong might have been thrilled at how easy it was to catch Ning Nong's supper, but the elephant was uncharacteristically edgy. He started acting strangely; Amber could sense Ning Nong's uneasiness. The beach was eerily calm, and Ning Nong did something he'd never done before. Instead of his usual gentle ramble, the elephant picked up speed. Although elephants might not move the 30 to 40 miles per hour a thoroughbred horse is able to gallop, when pushed, Asian elephants can move as fast as 15 miles per hour. Clearly, Amber found herself holding on for dear life if she didn't want to be tossed off Ning Nong's back, but she later told reporters that she wasn't afraid. Looking back on her ordeal, Amber felt the elephant knew she was in danger.

Thankfully, Ning Nong did know what he was doing, but elephants are a loyal lot, and his handler was still in danger. With a little extra encouragement from Yong, who by now was aware that disaster was imminent, the elephant followed its instincts and ran. Ning Nong rushed as far away from the shoreline as was possible.

"Everyone was running out of the sea, and my mum began crying because she thought she'd lost me," Amber told reporters from BBC News.

"If she had been on the beach on her own or with us on the beach, she would never have lived. The elephant took the pounding of the wave," Samantha added.

Amber and Ning Nong survived the first wave, but there were more to come. After Samantha collected Amber and rushed back to the hotel where the family was staying, another wave was cresting. By the time mother and daughter reached their hotel room, several neighboring rooms located closer to the beach were engulfed in water. The angry ocean had not yet calmed its ire.

In the days to come, the world heard eyewitness accounts of the catastrophic event and how, during the several hours when the tsunami reigned, the Indian Ocean would recede, sometimes a great many yards away from its normal shoreline, only to crest again, with walls of water reaching as high as 50 feet and roaring like a jet engine. Some people were pulled into the ocean when the waves abated while their loved ones next to them stumbled to safety. In the days and weeks to come, the grim task of collecting and disposing of any dead that could be recovered dominated everyone's energies. And still today, more than six years later, communities are still being rebuilt.

Amber and her family were among the lucky survivors.

Luck, Love or Instinct?

Many Phuket residents who saw the waters receding in the moments before the tsunami hit or who noticed animals that, on sensing what was to come, were getting anxious and heading for higher ground, also took their cue from Mother Nature and rushed their friends and family away from the seashore. They survived. But for others who were enjoying themselves and unaware of the danger signs, happenstance dealt a cruel blow.

On the whole, animals fared better than the human inhabitants. According to local legends, the animals knew the tsunami was coming—reportedly, very few dead animals were discovered after the tsunami. In a documentary produced about Amber's story and the devastating tsunami, Britain's Demand Five TV reported that Aniway Jong Kit, an elephant handler and owner of the Khao Lak Elephant Trekking Centre located some 50 miles from the beaches where Amber was playing with Ning Nong, reported that their elephants had acted strangely before the tsunami hit, shaking off their chains and rushing to higher ground.

"We couldn't stop the elephants," Jong Kit told NBC News correspondent Charles Sabine.

Kit was far from alone when it came to believing animals were more in tune with what was going to happen in their environment than their human counterparts. According to the *Washington Post*, one Danish man vacationing in Ao Sane Beach just north of Phuket shared his thoughts on a Danish website: "Dogs are smarter than all of us… [They] started running away up to the hilltops long before we even realized what was coming."

The media jumped into action defending the theory, quoting experts expounding on the claim. The *Washington Post* article spoke of how "Animals' sensory physiology—super-sensitive to sound, temperature, touch, vibration, electrostatic and chemical activity and magnetic fields—gives them a head start in the days and hours before natural calamities." Quoting George Pararas-Carayannis, former University of Hawaii oceanographer and geophysicist who, at the time, led the Tsunami Society, "It appears a lot of animals have sensory organs that detect these micro-tremors and micro-changes that we cannot possibly monitor."

Other scientists disagreed. Eric Wikramanayake of the Conservation Science Program, World Wildlife Fund in Washington, DC, and Peter Leimgruber of the National Zoological Park, Conservation and Research Centre in Front Royal, Virginia, had been conducting a study on the movements of satellite-collared elephants in Southern Sri Lanka before and after the December 2004 tsunami. On hearing the claims that animals, especially elephants, had some kind of "sixth sense" that warned them to get to higher ground before the waves hit, Wikramanayake and Leimgruber reviewed information collected from two radio-collared elephants the scientists had been studying. The collars were equipped with GPS technology, and the scientists were able to track the elephants' movements. They hypothesized that if elephants did have a sixth sense about the December 26 disaster, the elephants they were tracking would have moved farther inland during the tsunami than they had at any other time. However, the information they collected did not support that theory.

Controversial opinions about animal instincts weren't the only things experts disagreed upon. Another point of contention surrounded a plethora of stories where animals were credited with saving people from the tsunami. At one point, a story started circulating via chain-emails that appears to have its roots in the true stories of Amber's survival and the elephants breaking free of their chains at the Khao Lak Elephant Trekking Centre. The email story suggested that wandering elephants had purposely returned to Phuket's beaches and rescued more than 40 people.

The folks from Snopes.com blew a hole in that story, saying there was no proof of such a mass rescue effort. The Internet watchdog site did suggest that some stories of elephants rescuing people were true, but they were instances of coincidence—the individuals were already interacting with these animals and were saved because the elephants had been spooked and rushed to higher ground. Snopes.com also commented on the story of Amber and Ning Nong, calling it the "closest real instance to the rumor." Still, Snopes diminishes the miracle that the Masons believe was theirs to hold for all time, saying, "the elephant did not of its own accord rescue the endangered."

The Masons see it otherwise. In fact, they believe so strongly that Yong's beloved elephant knew what he was doing when he saved Amber that the couple pledged to donate £30 a month to contribute to his care for as long as Ning Nong lives. Since most well-cared-for elephants can live as long as 60 years, it's quite conceivable Amber will some day be making those payments.

Something tells me she won't mind in the least.

Not Just Another Pretty Face

Pretty is as pretty does.

–Author unknown

THEY'RE KNOWN FOR THEIR CUTE, cuddly appearance and their ability to rapidly procreate, but rabbits are smart, too. If you don't believe me, consider this report from Melbourne, Australia.

Gerry Keogh, a nightclub employee, was sliding into sleep in the early morning hours of July 24, 2008, while his partner, Michelle Finn, was trying to catch a few more zzzs before getting ready for her day, when their pet bunny named Rabbit woke the couple. "Gerry only got home from work about 5:30 AM because he works night shift, and about 7:00 AM, we both woke to the sound of a thumping rabbit," Finn told the *Brisbane Times*.

The couple barely had time to react to their rabbit's strange behavior when they heard windows breaking. They opened their bedroom door to a house filled with smoke and fire. It took 15 firefighters to douse the flames. With a house thick with smoke, firefighters had to wear breathing gear to rescue the hero bunny. It was later determined that an electrical heater had caused the fire.

Keogh and Finn had spent the better part of the previous two years renovating their house. As a result, the couple's fire alarm had been removed and deactivated. Had it not been for Rabbit's persistent commotion, the couple would have most likely perished.

In December 2006, a similar occurrence, this time in Sydney, Australia, resulted in a tabby cat saving a couple and their two children after a mattress caught fire. A spokesman for the fire department told reporters that they believed the fire was caused by a cigarette, but thanks to the cat's quick actions, no one was injured, and the family's home sustained minimal damage.

Part Four

PET BUDDIES

We are each of us angels with only one wing,
and we can fly only by embracing each other.

–Lucian De Crescenzo, Greek philosopher

I REMEMBER WHEN A CARELESS DRIVER killed my beautiful sheltie, Amadeus. I'd just put Amadeus and his buddy, Skyla, outside for a brief moment, and although we didn't have a fenced yard, the dogs never ventured off our property. Besides, I was standing at the back door overseeing them do their business, so I wasn't worried about anything untoward happening that day.

I'd only turned my head for a moment to respond to my young daughter when Amadeus was spooked by a truck rushing down our back lane. He must have done the unthinkable and charged toward the vehicle. Either way, in the split second it took to turn my head, the truck hit my black beauty. He didn't die at the scene; in fact, I really thought he'd only suffered a broken leg. But a trip to the veterinarian's confirmed the damage was irreparable, and we had to euthanize the loveliest dog we'd ever owned.

I was devastated. I felt responsible for turning my attention for such a brief moment. Our entire family mourned his loss, but perhaps no one more so than Skyla.

Amadeus was a year old when we adopted our second sheltie and was still young enough to appreciate having a new puppy around. But he made no bones about letting Skyla know who was top dog in our family. Skyla, on the other hand, bowed to every nod or growl, every glance or doggy grin Amadeus might toss her way. For example, when the two played catch, Skyla—the larger of the two dogs—always reached the ball first. Then, as if she knew what was expected of her, she'd step back from the ball and let Amadeus take it into his mouth and return it to the person who was playing with them at the time. Amadeus ate first, drank first, took the first treat, received the first pet and generally called all the shots in their little doggy world, and Skyla let him.

When Amadeus yelped that day after being hit by the car, Skyla went into shock. Her body shook uncontrollably, and for the next several days, when it became clear to her that Amadeus would not be coming home, she sat in solemn silence. For weeks she mourned and stared into the distance. She didn't eat. Barely drank. Didn't respond to a call for a walk.

I'd heard of this kind of bond between animals but had never witnessed it before. And although Skyla wasn't called to any act of heroism surrounding Amadeus' unfortunate plight, the grief she demonstrated to the loss of her buddy was a clear indication of her affection for him. I've no doubt that were she able to do anything in her power to change what happened, she would have.

The stories in this section reveal that kind of love between animals, and the many faces of heroism made manifest in their actions toward each other.

Dogs, Dogs, Dogs

I believe that unarmed truth and unconditional love will have the final word in reality. This is why right, temporarily defeated, is stronger than evil triumphant.

–Martin Luther King Jr., Civil Rights leader and Baptist minister

Fast Friends, Loving Hearts

To care for anyone else enough to make their problems one's own, is ever the beginning of one's real ethical development.

–Felix Adler, religious leader and social reformer

HEROES AREN'T JUST MADE UP OF brave people doing dangerous and inexplicable feats with the sole purpose of helping someone else and with no thought to their own safety. A hero is also defined as an individual who is "admired for his brave deeds *and* noble qualities." Noble qualities include an "exalted moral or mental character or excellence." Perhaps nothing is more noble or, by default, heroic, than an individual who puts themselves out to bring joy to another.

You might believe that animals are capable of exhibiting noble qualities such as these to their human buddies, but what about befriending their own species?

Seeing a dog roam about aimlessly on a city street might not be desirable, but it's not uncommon. Dogs wandering around the countryside are fairly typical as well. But when you notice a pair of pups shuffling about unattended for a day or so, and you don't know to whom they belong and there's no clear indication anyone will claim them, it might be time to call the local animal rescue folks to come down and have a look.

That's exactly what happened in July 2009 near the community of Blundeston, Norfolk, in the United Kingdom. Early that month, residents in the area noticed a pair of black-and-white border collies walking without any apparent purpose in the middle of a rainstorm. It seemed reasonable to assume that the typically intelligent collies wouldn't have chosen to be outside in the rain, and so it was theorized the pair was either lost or abandoned.

The dogs' behavior was a bit odd as well, with one dog always following the other in a peculiar sort of way, occasionally placing its head on the leading dog's backside as the pair made its way down the street. This added to folks' concern. At one point, a local resident driving her car past the two strays stopped and opened her door. Surprisingly, the dogs didn't hesitate for a second and jumped in. The woman took them to the local authorities, and they were placed at the Meadow Green Dog Rescue Centre in nearby Loddon until their owners could be located.

It didn't take long for Cherie Cootes and her mother, Sue, the duo who manages the rescue centre, to recognize what it was about the two dogs that made them so unique. Neither dog had any identifiable markings, microchips, collars or tags, so they were soon named Bonnie and Clyde because they were inseparable. But that wasn't the most amazing part of this duo. It was soon discovered that five-year-old Clyde, the larger, longhaired collie, was blind due to a degenerative eye disease. Two-year-old Bonnie, the smaller, shorthaired collie, had taken on the responsibility of being Clyde's guide dog.

"She's a little darling, and he just follows her everywhere," Sue told reporters from *The Daily Telegraph*. "It's just instinctive with them to help each other, and it's marvelous to see animals doing this together."

Sue went on to explain that Clyde's habit of placing his head on Bonnie's haunches seems to help to center him when he becomes confused. When the two dogs were out and about in the yard, Sue noticed that Bonnie frequently stopped walking to make sure Clyde was close behind. The self-trained pup was acting as Clyde's seeing-eye dog. It was a strange scenario, even to Vicky Bell, spokesperson for Guide Dogs for the Blind

Association, but she acknowledged that some dogs are naturals at the job because of their calm disposition.

Bonnie certainly fit that criterion.

A public plea for the owner to claim the dogs didn't yield any results, and so Sue and Cherie went to the media in the hope of sharing the pair's story and encouraging the right person to come forward with an offer to adopt the pups. The problem was that Sue was adamant that the pair not be split up. She told reporters that Clyde was almost completely dependent on Bonnie to such an extent that he wouldn't move without sensing her nearby. Although there was no proof to the theory, it seemed reasonable to assume that the two dogs had lived together for quite some time, perhaps Bonnie's entire lifetime, prior to their discovery, and Sue was not about to separate them.

Another consideration the rescue center had to think about when placing the animals was the kind of environment they might require. Sue and Cherie believed the dogs, like most border collies, needed room to run, either in a large fenced yard or on a rural acreage or farm to eliminate the possibility of Clyde getting hit by a car. Bonnie also needed space to safely run and burn off some of that teenaged energy.

The Cootes women were pleased by the response they received to the stories appearing in *The Daily Telegraph*, *BBC*, *The Daily Mail* and other area media.

More than 500 offers to adopt the dogs poured into the rescue shelter. In the end, Bonnie and Clyde went to live with an "experienced dog owner," and they now live in the countryside.

For now, the Cootes can turn their attention to the more than 40 abandoned dogs they typically care for at their shelter at any given time. Each of these pups is special, and Sue and Cherie work hard to adapt them to a new environment and find them good homes. But for these women, along with anyone who heard about the story, it's quite likely that this Bonnie and Clyde duo will hold a special place in their hearts.

As far as Clyde goes, Bonnie is certainly his hero, but I'd bet that Bonnie thinks similarly of Clyde. After all, he's given the girl a job to do and a buddy with which to wander the road of life.

Risking All for a Stranger

True heroism is remarkably sober, very undramatic. It is not the urge to surpass all others at whatever cost, but the urge to serve others at whatever cost.

–Arthur Ashe, social activist and former professional tennis player

IT'S NOT CLEAR WHAT LED TO THE separation of one Heinz-57 variety dog from its master, but this nameless mongrel didn't let a little thing like temporary homelessness detract from his character. In March 2009, the large-breed dog, which looked part German shepherd, noticed a fellow canine in distress on the Santiago freeway in Chile and rushed to the rescue—and it required him to run through several lanes of high-way traffic to accomplish the feat. The dog on the receiving end of the rescue was about the same size as its rescuer and had wandered into the traffic and been hit by a car just moments before.

The hero dog witnessed the accident and hurried along the highway median to the wounded dog's aid. The video obtained from a nearby traffic camera showed how the rescue dog placed his paws on either side of the fallen dog's chest and neck and inched his way backwards across the traffic, dragging the injured dog in front of him. Sadly, the injured dog passed away, but he died without suffering any further injuries.

Remarkably, several versions of the rescue were posted on YouTube shortly after it happened. Altogether, the versions have garnered almost a million views, and the story made news around the world.

Unfortunately, the hero of this story seems to have vanished without a trace.

Open Adoption

It's better to have a loving family than to have no family at all.

–Author unknown

FRIENDLY. KIND. THE MOST HONEST breed you'll ever find. These are some of the descriptors used by folks who know and love golden retrievers. Perhaps the next story, which might seem strange to some of us, serves as a concrete example of the familiar claims about the breed's temperament.

In February 2010, Barbara Thoma welcomed a baby female lamb onto her Cooper County, Missouri farm. New animals are usually a cause for celebration for farming folks, but this lamb was inordinately small. Disturbed to see that the lamb's mother had rejected it, Thoma decided to set up a cozy corner in the garage and nurse along the lamb herself. Little did she know she'd have help from an unexpected source—her golden retriever, Rosie. As cheery as her name implies, Rosie took right over, loving the lamb as if it were one of her pups. The lamb responded to the dog's kindness and even started taking on some of the retriever's behaviors, such as sneaking in and out of the Thomas home via the doggy door.

Needless to say, the Thoma family is quite happy with the lamb's progress, though they've had to work at reintegrating the tot back with others of its own kind.

Feisty Felines

I believe cats to be spirits come to earth.

A cat, I am sure, could walk on a cloud without coming through.

—Jules Verne, author

No Sacrifice Too Great

Before you were conceived I wanted you,
Before you were born I loved you
Before you were here an hour I would die for you
This is the miracle of life.

—Maureen Hawkins, writer

BY MARCH, THE WEATHER IN BROOKLYN, New York, is starting to recover from the cool, damp and sometimes blustery winter months. Average temperatures hover around 50° F during the day and 35° F in the evening—certainly not hot by any stretch of the imagination, but it verges on comfortable. On warmer days, the grass struggles to shoot forth fresh, green spears to replace the brown ones of fall, and buds are starting to form on the trees. Everywhere you turn, even in the most dilapidated back lanes of an inner city neighborhood, the miracle of life is unfolding.

This season of new birth saw another of life's miracles in March 1996. Tucked away in the corner of an abandoned garage, a mother calico cat was tending to her youngsters. There were five of them—two black-and-whites, a white fluff ball, a gray with white markings and a fawn-colored mongrel. None of them looked like the mother tending them, but they were hers, each and every last one of them, and she tended to those kittens like they were of purebred stock. By this time, the four-week-old kittens all had their eyes open and were becoming increasingly aware of their surroundings. But they were still a little wobbly on their legs and depended on mamma cat for food and liquids as well as protection from danger.

The weather was a little cooler than usual on the night of March 30. In fact, it was freezing cold, and mama cat settled down for the night, curling up around her babies to keep them warm. For some reason though, she couldn't relax. Somehow she sensed all was not well with her world. After a while, smoke began to fill the garage she called home, and it wasn't long before the calico noticed a growing fire, intensifying by the minute, rapidly begin to consume the building.

Mama cat knew she didn't have much time if she wanted to save herself and her babies from the searing flames. They were at that awkward age—too large to carry two at a time but too young to rush them out of the building on their own steam. And so she grabbed one of her litter by the scruff of its neck and headed outside.

Sounding the Alarm

When the call came into Ladder Company 175 Brooklyn, firefighters wasted no time in responding. They'd been called out to the area several times before, and they knew the building in question. It was a shack made up of dried boards and splintered wood, and some reports suggested it was used from time to time as crack house. Since a fire would devour the structure in short order, firefighters knew they had to move fast just in case there were people in the otherwise deserted shell.

Once they arrived, it didn't take the smoke jumpers long to contain the blaze. When the threat of the fire spreading to neighboring buildings was no longer a concern, firefighter David Gianelli took a look around at the pile of charred remains. He didn't find any human casualties, which was certainly a plus. He did, however, hear something that sounded like an animal or animals in distress—having been nicknamed "the animal guy" by his colleagues, the 17-year veteran with the unit knew a hurting and frightened animal when he heard one.

Turning in the direction of the whines, he noticed a scruffy-looking cat hobbling out of the scorched building with what looked like a kitten in her mouth. The cat dropped the tot a safe distance away and, after meowing a few orders, turned and rushed back into the heat and smoke of what was once the feline family's home. By the time Gianelli reached the mama cat, she'd managed to rescue all five of her babies and was in the process of nosing up each one of them, as if she was counting to make sure she'd gotten everyone to safety before resting long enough to lick her own wounded body.

Photographs of the cat taken in the days following the incident showed the extent to which this young mother, who was believed to be no more than a year old and raising her first litter, went to save her youngsters. Gianelli's description of Scarlett, as the world would come to know the cat, fleshed the image out even further. The cat's fur was singed and patchy, her skin burned to such an extent that her ears looked deformed, her whiskers were burnt off, and her paws were raw. Veterinarians at the North Shore Animal League in Port Washington, New York, where Gianelli had taken the family, cleaned and dressed the ailing mother. Her eyes were so damaged that they were blistered over—it was later surmised that Scarlett used her nose to count her kittens after the fire because she couldn't see them. Scarlett's selfless act of courage and devotion stirred a nation, and the story touched the hearts of people around the globe.

Through her actions, Scarlett became the very embodiment of motherly love.

The Rest of the Story

Some sources suggest that after the fire that thrust the plight of Scarlett and her kittens into the public spotlight, the North Shore Animal League received as many as 7000 letters from concerned animal lovers sending their get-well wishes and offering to adopt Scarlett or one of her four surviving kittens. It took three months of ongoing medical care for Scarlett and her youngsters to recover from their injuries. Sadly, the smallest of the litter, a white snowdrop of a thing, developed a virus when it was about eight weeks old and just didn't have the strength to battle through another assault on its tiny body.

When it was time for the family to go to their new homes, the kittens that staff named Oreo and Smokey went out to a family in Miller Place, Long Island. Samsara and Panuki, siblings that had been inseparable since their rescue from the fire, left to live with a Port Washington family. That left Scarlett waiting to be claimed by her new owner, Karen Wellen—Wellen had been chosen as Scarlett's adoptive mom after the North Shore Animal League heard how the woman had survived a car crash and had lost her own cat.

While the mom and her kittens were off living good lives in their new homes, the captivating story of a mother who returned over and over again into a burning building despite her own raw and scorched skin that burned with each exposure to the heat, never ceased to stir people's hearts. Scarlett appeared on CNN and *Oprah* as well as in news articles as far away as Japan. Two books were eventually written about Scarlett: a children's book by Laura Driscoll, *The Bravest Cat!*, and *Scarlett Saves Her Family* by Jane Martin. The brave mother was also featured in a book entitled *Cat Book*, by Emily Eve Weinstein.

Weinstein visited Scarlett five years after the fire and described how the feline still bore the scars of that terrible day. There were "deep scars on her legs and feet," her face was nearly hairless, and her "oddly upturned eyes and nubbed ears [bore] witness to her ordeal." But the cat had gained weight, managing to tip the scales at 16 pounds, and her coat was full and healthy. And she was happy, too. According to Wellen, the Brooklyn native couldn't have asked for a better companion. Scarlett was playful and cuddly, and "the most lovable cat in the world."

For the next 12 years, Scarlett enjoyed a relatively stress-free life in her new home. Then in October 2008, Scarlett's story hit the media outlets once again. At the age of 13, the cat that captured the hearts of cat lovers everywhere, said her last farewell. She'd lived a long life considering the ongoing care she needed as a result of her injuries.

Near the end of her days, Scarlett was diagnosed with a heart murmur, kidney failure and lymphoma. Wellen sang "You Are So Beautiful" as Scarlett was being put down. "She went peacefully in my arms. I told her how much I loved her," Wellen told reporters, explaining how the cat's ashes now sit on Scarlett's favorite windowsill "where she always looked out."

Shortly after Scarlett and her kittens recovered from the injuries they sustained during the fire, the North Shore Animal League established the Scarlett Award for Animal Heroism. The calico also became what the center calls a Pet Representative—"symbolic animals that represent all the real and wonderful dogs and cats in North Shore Animal League America's Sponsor Program."

According to its website, the North Shore Animal League America is "the world's largest no-kill animal rescue and adoption organization." It was established in 1944. Since its inception, the organization has rescued and found homes for almost one million dogs and cats.

Scarlett was truly one in a million.

Other Critters We Love

An animal's eyes have the power to speak a great language.

–Martin Buber, philosopher

Mother Heart Helps Others
with Second Chance

Out of difficulties grow miracles.

–Jean de La Bruyere, French essayist

ALONE. THE DARK, GRIMY GARDEN shed was devoid of any creature comforts. It was cold. There was no food or water anywhere. And aside from the frightened, young greyhound cowering in a corner, it was bereft of any life.

The terrified dog was alone.

There's no clear indication how long this deprived canine had been locked away like a bag of kitchen garbage in a deserted shack in Warwickshire, England, and there were no reports regarding her history, but by the time police broke into the shack, the dog was in pretty bad shape. She was dust-covered and much of her body was coated in mud. She'd been beaten. And she was malnourished, her already lean frame emaciated to such an extent it was hard to imagine her surviving. It would take a miracle of veterinary medicine, and a strong will on the dog's part, if she were to overcome her ordeal physically. How the experience would affect her temperament wasn't something anyone could predict.

No one would have guessed they were breathing new life into a dog that would soon become a hero to other abandoned, abused and stray animals.

About Greyhounds

The greyhound's history can be traced back 8000 years: that's the estimated age of many of the primitive sketches of the breed lining the walls of several primeval caves. The greyhound's lineage dates back to the ancient Egyptians, and these dogs, which were both docile and useful, were companions and hunting partners to all manner of royalty. The breed's long, lean body gifted the animal with the ability to outrun most other species of canine, reaching speeds of as high as 45 miles per hour.

It's little wonder, then, that the greyhound was eventually groomed for speed. The thought was that training these dogs to race on a track similar to a horse track and betting on the outcome was as exciting as horse racing. For some folks, racing greyhounds is even a larger draw—it takes a lot less money to feed a greyhound. The problem was that most greyhounds are past their racing prime between the ages of two and six, and because a greyhound can live to be 12 to 14 years old, that leaves racing enthusiasts with a problem: what can be done with the retired dogs? And there are a lot of retired greyhounds.

A system was eventually developed by some less-than-scrupulous owners to relinquish the animals to veterinarians to be euthanized. But that costs money, and so some owners of these beautiful creatures took to either killing their dogs themselves or paying a middleman half the cost of a vet to do their dirty work for them. In one widely reported case coming from Lillian, Alabama, an individual was convicted of animal torture after it was discovered he had as many as 3000 greyhounds—dogs he'd admitted to killing over a 40-year period—buried on his 18-acre farm.

Today, there are checks and balances put in place by the greyhound racing industry and animal pro-tection agencies to prevent such abuses, but they still happen from time to time. It's not clear if this particular greyhound discovered in the locked garden shed in the Midlands region of England was once a racing greyhound, but it had been disposed of with just as much cruelty.

The Road to Healing

Once the police were able to coax the trembling animal into their care, they took it directly to the Nuneaton Warwickshire Wildlife Sanctuary where owner Geoff Grewcock and his staff took over. The sanctuary started out as a refuge for a wounded swan in June 2000 and evolved into a full-scale animal refuge by February 2001. In the preceding years, Grewcock and his helpers had seen animals injured by motor vehicles, mangled by fishing lines, shot by hunters but not killed, or lost and abandoned, but they were still mortified by this dog's condition. It was clear the animal's new caregivers would have to gain her trust with every attempt to wash her, groom her or dress her wounds. True to the organization's mission of "improving the lives of animals, one at a time" in whatever way is needed, staff poured their hearts into her care.

Of course, the poor pup needed a name, and so it was decided to call her Jasmine, a befitting moniker for such a beautiful and delicate creature.

Jasmine's physical scars healed fairly quickly and she started to gain weight, but it took a little longer for the dog to relinquish her anxiety and trust her caregivers completely. Abuse quite often breeds abusers, but it was rapidly apparent that this particular pup was a gentle soul. She revealed her sweet disposition early on in her care and continued to blossom as the days and weeks went on.

Most animals brought to the sanctuary are nursed back to health, reintegrated with other animals and people, and eventually placed in suitable adoptive homes.

But it soon became clear that Jasmine had no intention of moving on.

The Mother Heart

Foxes and dogs don't usually get along. Although a fox is wild, and a dog is domesticated, a dog is viewed as a fox's natural predator. Hunters have paired up with hounds in organized foxhunts in England since the early 1500s and in ancient Egypt, Babylonia and Assyria many hundreds of years before that. At some point in foxhunt history, the greyhound was introduced as a sight hound because of the breed's exceptional vision and was used to spot a wild animal and initiate the hunt. Given the relationship between dogs and foxes, no one expected what occurred when a young kit named Roxy moved into the Nuneaton Warwickshire Wildlife Sanctuary.

Jasmine's talents at mothering first became evident when one of the staff members at the sanctuary noticed the dog's interest in the orphaned kit. Jasmine licked young Roxy, picked her up by the scruff of her neck, carried her to a location Jasmine felt was safe for such a youngster and snuggled up beside her. Roxy responded to Jasmine's attention, licking her new mama almost as much as Jasmine licked Roxy.

Although it was a little unusual to see one of the animals at the refuge take such an ardent interest in another, it wasn't altogether unlikely. But Jasmine didn't stop with Roxy. Not long after that, the sanctuary acquired two abandoned puppies: a Lakeland terrier cross and a Jack Russell Doberman cross. "They were tiny when they arrived at the centre, and Jasmine approached them and grabbed one by the scruff of the neck in her mouth and put him on the settee," Grewcock told reporters from Britain's *Daily Mail*. "Then she fetched the other one and sat down with them, cuddling them."

Jasmine's mothering instinct grew with every new animal that entered the refuge. She'd greet these tenderfoots with a stroke of her snout or a lick behind the ears, curl up beside them, often in a bed of her own making, and act as all-round protector. As Grewcock put it, Jasmine had the ability to take all the stress out of these poor creatures, and that helped in their healing and the adjustment to their new surroundings.

Jasmine not only won the hearts of every stray and injured animal at the sanctuary, but she also wormed her way into the hearts of everyone who worked there. Jasmine had effectively graduated from the ranks of the "adoptable" to that of the "adopted." She was home. And she'd never be alone again.

The Rescue Work Continues

Since her arrival in 2003, and as of this writing, Jasmine has adopted 50 animals. Despite what some might suggest are the laws of nature—that birds and bunnies are usually a little shy of dogs—Jasmine has endeared herself to every species of bird or animal lodging at the sanctuary. Bunnies and guinea pigs, badger cubs and baby chicks all have gladly accepted Jasmine's mothering. Even birds have perched on the bridge of her nose without Jasmine batting an eye over the situation.

"She simply dotes on the animals as if they were her own, it's incredible to see," Grewcock told several news sources. "Having been neglected herself, it's a real surprise to see her show so much warmth and affection to other creatures."

In February 2009, Jasmine adopted her 50th foster child—a tiny, 11-week-old roe deer fawn that staff at the refuge had named Bramble. A man out walking his dog discovered the semiconscious fawn in a field not far from the sanctuary. As soon as Bramble arrived, Jasmine was on full alert, licking her clean and keeping her warm.

"They are inseparable at the moment, Bramble walks between her legs, and they keep kissing each other," Geoff told the *Daily Mail*. "They walk together round the sanctuary. It's absolutely marvelous. It's a real treat to see them."

Eventually, Bramble will be released back into the wild; it's where she belongs.

At the age of seven, Jasmine is well into her projected lifespan, but she has no time for slowing down. Once Bramble is off, nibbling leaves in the wild and chasing butterflies, Jasmine will no doubt have another orphan to nurse back to health. It's her destiny.

It's strange how sometimes, when life seems blackest and turned all upside down, a ray of hope shines through and makes things better than they'd ever been before. Had Jasmine never been rescued that night in 2003, the young greyhound would have never had the chance to realize her full potential. The world would have been a sadder place had that been the case.

As it turned out, Jasmine will never be alone again. She has a job to do that seems to give her a sense of self-worth, and she brings joy to everyone around her. Most importantly, she has a place to call home.

Afterword

Anyone who has ever known and loved a dog will attest to the animal's unwavering faithfulness, its ability to always know when something is bothering its owner and its seemingly unending capacity to both give and receive affection. But as hard as it might seem to those of us who are dog lovers, the beloved canine isn't necessarily the pet of choice for everyone. In the United States, 4 in 10 households own a dog, and with about 68 million pet dogs in the country, about 24 percent of those households own more than one.

Cats run a close second when it comes to the favorite pet of choice, with 3 in 10 American households owning at least one cat. However, the feline outnumbers its canine competition with 73 million cats owned in the U.S. and 51 percent of cat-loving households owning two or more cats.

The number of dog and cat owners in Canada isn't as clearly tracked as it is in the United States. However, a 2002 survey out of Leger Marketing Express, the largest independent research firm in Canada, suggests that about 53 percent of Canadians own a pet. Thirty percent of those pet owners have a dog, 28 percent have a cat, and 10 percent own some other type of animal. About "32 percent of dog owners also own a cat and 15 percent have another type of pet."

Another survey suggests that although seniors and retirees might think twice about adopting a new pet, citing a desire to travel and visit family as one of the biggest reasons for the choice, it appears pet ownership is on the rise. The *Canadian Veterinary Journal* noted that in 2008, pet ownership in Canada had increased to 56 percent of the population; those numbers were echoed in 2007 when the Canadian Animal Health Institute partnered with Ipsos Reid with a survey of its own. According to their numbers, there were 7.9 million cats and 5.9 million dogs living in Canada. As in the United States, most Canadian pet-owning households still have dogs, but cat lovers often have more than one cat, which is why there are more cats than dogs in Canada.

In some cases, the choice between owning a cat or a dog has a lot to do with an individual's personality. An active, outdoorsy kind of person looking for companionship on the road, or someone to pair up with on mountain hikes or evening jogs, might prefer a dog. On the other hand, an individual who enjoys the presence of animal company but requires a pet of a more independent nature might prefer to own a cat.

When it comes to uncovering how we interact with our furry friends, another study showed that pets rank so high in our lives that some folks (one in 10 women) are willing to sacrifice all, even a relationship, for their pet. These critters aren't just animals, they're family members, especially in a woman's mind, and almost 60 percent of female pet owners would risk their lives to save their pet. About 28 percent of the time, an animal's needs are placed before its owner's needs, and more than one news story has outlined how seniors have been known to go without food in order to spend their meager pension on feeding their cats and dogs. And if you've ever stopped by a household with children bereft of a gerbil, puppy, canary or fish, chances are the youngsters are begging for one.

Cats and dogs aren't the only options for animal lovers looking for companions of the unconditional variety. Birds have been the pets of choice for more than 4000 years. As with the cat, Egyptians were credited as the first civilization to keep these pets. Exotic birds, such as parrots and cockatiels, can have quite the entertaining personalities, chirping out the odd phrase or two they pick up from their human owners. Canaries bring joy with their wispy songs, and birds of other varieties are pretty to look at. Exotic fish are also therapeutic for that same reason: they are beautiful to focus on, a way to relax after a hectic day.

Whether your pet is a guinea pig, a ferret, a gecko or a snake, studies have shown that people who live with animals have lower blood pressure and cholesterol, heal from injury and illness more quickly and have an overall better quality of life than people without animals.

For nonbelievers, when it comes to recognizing the unique personalities and amazing abilities of our pets, crediting these creatures with anything other than an animal instinct to survive is simply ludicrous.

Pet lovers, however, know full well the depth of faithfulness an animal companion is capable of providing. Just as we know when our pet is hungry, needs to relieve itself or wants a walk or a belly rub, our pets know us, too. They sense when something is bothering us. They recognize our mood swings. They're fiercely protective—I dare you to try to get inside my home without our two shelties attacking you! And they're stubbornly loyal.

St. Francis of Assisi once said that, "Not to hurt our humble brethren (the animals) is our first duty to them, but to stop there is not enough. We have a higher mission—to be of service to them whenever they require it... If you have men who will exclude any of God's creatures from the shelter of compassion and pity, you will have men who will deal likewise with their fellow men." After all the care and compassion and faithful dedication our pets have shown to us throughout the ages, this is the very least we must do.

Notes on Sources

A BOOK LIKE THIS DOESN'T COME together without the legwork of a great many journalists, broadcasters, bloggers and folklorists. What follows is a selection of the many sources drawn upon in the creation of these stories.

ASSOCIATIONS AND NEWS AGENCIES

ABC News

Alaska State Troopers (press release)

Asian News International

Associated Press

Bali Times

Baltimore Daily Record (The)

Bay City News

Big Wave TV

BBC News

Canada's Guide to Dogs

Canadian Press

Canwest News Service

CBC News

Chilliwack Progress

CNN News

Courthouse Dogs, LLC

CTV News

Daily Mail

Demand Five TV

Dumfries and Galloway Constabulary

El Paso Times

Encyclopedia Britannica

Foundation for Service Dog Support, Inc.

Global TV BC

Hamilton Spectator

Huffington Post

The Humane Society of the United States

KTVU.com

Mail Foreign Service

MSN News

National Geographic News

National Post

NBC News

North American Police Work Dog Association

The Oakland Tribune

People magazine

People's Dispensary for Sick Animals

Police Dog Service Training Centre, Depot Division

The Province

Purina Animal Hall of Fame

QMI Agency

RCMP Police Dog Services

Reuters News Agency

RIA Novosti, Russian news-wire service

Silver City Sun-News

The Telegraph, UK

The Thai India News

Throng TV

United States Police Canine Association

USA Today

Vancouver Sun

WEBSITES

www.digitaljournal.com

www.examiner.com

www.exoticpets.about.com

www.greyhoundnetworknews.org

www.gulfcoastgreyhounds.org

jetofiada.tripod.com/Story.htm

www.maritimequest.com/warship_directory/great_britain/pages/sloops/hms_amethyst_u16_able_seacat_simon.htm

www.nationalzoo.si.edu/Publications/SWcientificPublications/pdfs/41A3412A-04F5-48D1-86A7-8BF03813F28B.pdf

www.npca.net (National Police Canine Association)

www.nuneatonwildlife.com

www.nydailynews.com

www.oklahoma4h.okstate.edu

www.petcareclub.com

www.post-gazette.com

www.purr-n-fur.org.uk/famous/simon/html

www.thestar.com

www.startribune.com

www.warwickshirewildlifesanctuary.co.uk

www.wikipedia.org

Lisa Wojna

Lisa Wojna, author of several other non-fiction books, has worked in the community newspaper industry as a writer and journalist and has traveled all over Canada, from the windy prairies of Manitoba to northern British Columbia, and even to the wilds of Africa. Although writing and photography have been a central part of her life for as long as she can remember, it's the people behind every story that are her motivation and give her the most fulfillment.